THE AMERICAN TROJAN HORSE

THE AMERICAN TROJAN HORSE

U.S. Television Confronts Canadian Economic and Cultural Nationalism

BARRY BERLIN

Contributions to the Study of Mass Media and Communications, Number 22
Bernard K. Johnpoll, Series Editor

Greenwood Press
New York • Westport, Connecticut • London

Library of Congress Cataloging-in-Publication Data

Berlin, Barry.
  The American Trojan horse : U.S. television confronts Canadian
economic and cultural nationalism / Barry Berlin.
    p. cm.—(Contributions to the study of mass media and
communications, ISSN 0732-4456 ; no. 22)
  Includes bibliographical references.
  ISBN 0-313-27508-4 (lib. bdg. : alk. paper)
  1. Television advertising—United States—Finance. 2. Television
advertising—Canada—Finance. 3. Investments, Canadian—United
States. 4. Television advertising—Law and legislation—Canada.
5. Television broadcasting policy—Canada. 6. Television
broadcasting policy—United States. I. Title. II. Title: Cultural
nationalism. III. Series.
HF6146.T42B44   1990
659.14′3′09730971—dc20   90-3338

British Library Cataloguing in Publication Data is available.

Library of Congress Catalog Card Number: 90-3338
ISBN: 0-313-27508-4
ISSN: 0732-4456

First published in 1990

Greenwood Press, 88 Post Road West, Westport, CT 06881
An imprint of Greenwood Publishing Group, Inc.

Printed in the United States of America

The paper used in this book complies with the
Permanent Paper Standard issued by the National
Information Standards Organization (Z39.48-1984).

10 9 8 7 6 5 4 3 2 1

Contents

Acknowledgments

In an undertaking of this kind, there are many who should be thanked. I want to express special appreciation to W. J. Howell, Jr., of Canisius College, Buffalo, for helping me to see the border "war" as a significant research topic; to Mary Cassata of the State University of New York at Buffalo, for encouraging my interest in matters Canadian; to Leslie G. Arries, Jr., former president of WIVB-TV in Buffalo, for full access to records of the U.S. border stations as they relate to this issue and for unfailing graciousness; to officials of Canada's Department of Communication and the Canadian Radio-television and Telecommunications Commission, Ottawa, for their cooperation and views; to Paula Kirsch of Canisius College, for her energy and efficiency in preparing the manuscript; and to my wife, Kinsey, for her tolerance and empathy with the lengthy project.

Part I
Background

1
Mass Media in Canada and the United States

Historically, Canada and the United States have had a complex and usually cordial relationship, based, in part, on common elements: a five-thousand-mile border; the same language for most of the population; democratic principles that evolved from the British; defense; personal, family, academic, and trade union ties; and trade and investment. Economically, they are each other's largest supplier, and customer, of goods. Americans have more money invested in Canada, over $70 billion in direct and portfolio investment, than anywhere else, and Canadians have more money invested in the United States, over $13 billion, than anywhere else.[1] Additionally, they are each other's major attraction. More than seventy-three million border crossings occur annually.[2]

As in any close relationship, however, there are instances of discord. One of the most emotional conflicts between these North American neighbors involves mass communication. The Canadian-U.S. television advertising border dispute has embroiled twenty-four U.S. television stations south of the border, principally the three network-affiliated stations in Buffalo and one in Bellingham, Washington (see Table 1), in a protracted dispute with Canada.[3] Termed "the border war" by the press, it centers on an estimated $20 million a year Canadian companies had spent in seeking to reach the Canadian audience through advertising on U.S. stations along the border. When Canada implemented measures in the 1970's to retain the $20 million, it led to a protracted international dispute that has involved several administrations both in Washington, D.C., and Ottawa, Ontario.[4]

TABLE 1

UNITED STATES BORDER TELEVISION STATIONS AND LICENSEES THAT HAVE BEEN DIRECTLY INVOLVED IN THE TRANS-BORDER AD DISPUTE

Station	Licensee (Owner)*
KVOS-TV, Bellingham, WA.	KVOS Television Corp. (parent company: Wotmeco Enterprises, Inc.**
WIVB-TV (formerly WBEN), Buffalo, NY	Buffalo Broadcasting, Inc.(parent company: Howard Publications, Inc).
WGR-TV, Buffalo, NY	Taft Broadcasting Company
WKBW-TV, Buffalo, NY	Capital Cities Communications, Inc.
WCAX-TV, Burlington, NY	Mt. Mansfield Television, Inc.
WPTZ-TV, North Pole, NY	Rolling Telecasting, Inc.
WAGM-TV, Presque Isle, ME	Aroostook Broadcasting Corp.
WABI-TV, Bangor, ME	Community Broadcasting Service
WICU-TV, Erie, PA	Great Lakes Communications, Inc.
KBJR-TV, Superior, WI	RJR Communications, Inc.
WPBN-TV & WTOM-TV, Inc. Cheboygan, MI	Midwestern Television Company (WTOM-TV)
WVII-TV, Bangor, ME	Eastern Maine Broadcasting System,Inc.

TABLE 1 (continued)

Station	Licensee (Owner)*
WDAZ-TV, Grand Forks-Devils Lake, ND	WDAY, Inc.
WDEE-TV, Erie, PA	Great Lakes Television Co.
WWNY-TV, Watertown, NY	Johnson Newspaper Corporation (formerly known as the Brockway Company)
KXLY-TV, Spokane, WA	Spokane TV, Inc.
KTHI-TV, Fargo, ND	Spokane TV, Inc.
KCFW-TV, Kalispell, MT	KMSO-TV, Inc.
KFBB-TV, Great Falls, MT	Advance Corporation
WEZF-TV, Burlington, VT	International Television Corp.
WSEE-TV, Erie, PA	Gillet Broadcasting of Pennsylvania, Inc.
KXMD-TV, Williston, ND	KXMC-TV, Inc.
KXMC-TV, Minot, ND	KXMC-TV, Inc.

Sources: Compiled from border stations legal papers in actions in regard to the Trade Act of 1974 and 1979 (See Complaint Filed Pursuant to Section 301 Committee of the Office of the Special Representative for Trade Negotiations, Washington, D.C., August 29, 1978; Comments of Certain U.S. Border Stations in the Matter of the Petition by Certain U.S. Television Licenses Alleging Certain Unfair Trade Practices by the Government of Canada. Before the Section 301 Committee, Office of the Special Representative for Trade Negotiations, November 29, 1978).

*In some cases, by 1988, some of the licensees have changed; in Buffalo, all three stations had new owners.

**Bellingham is one of at least two U.S. border stations that serve a minimum U.S. market and are aimed at a mass Canadian market. A second was in Pembina, North Dakota, population 200. The station had nearly twelve times the market near Winnepeg than its 65,000 living within the U.S.

5

The dispute evolved in two stages. The first, from 1970 to 1976, involved Canada enacting two measures to retain the estimated $20 million in advertising Canadian companies were placing on U.S. stations south of the border. The second stage, from 1976 to mid-1988, involved massive efforts by the United States border stations to have Canada remove, or substantially modify, barriers to their receiving advertising monies.

Stage one was sanctioned by Canada's broadcast regulatory agency, the Canadian Radio-television and Telecommunications Commission (CRTC). Three cable companies deleted commercials from border station programs while relaying the programs for Canadian distribution.[5] The move sparked threats by Buffalo stations to jam programming to Canada.[6] The border stations appealed unsuccessfully to the Canadian supreme court to bar the practice of deleting commercials.[7] Deletions were, however, largely suspended in 1976 when the Canadian parliament approved a tax law, Bill C-58, that disallowed tax deductions to Canadian companies that advertised on U.S. border station shows seen in Canada.[8]

Significantly deterring the advertising flow to border stations, Bill C-58 sparked a wide range of retaliatory measures by the border stations designed to get Canada to modify it. The strategy involved lobbying the U.S. Congress for both negotiation and retaliation, where the retaliation was often linked to bilateral irritants not directly connected to the border dispute. For example, two of the major efforts have been:

1. The border stations were able to have a tax exemption to Canada for United States conventions in Canada held hostage[9] in Congress for four years, a move that the Canadian tourist industry has said cost Canada $100 million a year.[10]

2. The border stations successfully claimed a violation of the Trade Act of 1974.[11] This led to presidents Carter and Reagan recommending that Congress pass legislation mirroring Bill C-58. The legislation, after years of lobbying by the border station, was enacted in the fall of 1984. It was expected to cost two Canadian broadcast stations in Windsor an estimated $5 million in lost advertising from the Detroit market.[12]

The conflict has four major interrelated roots. A central one lies in Canadian nationalism, particularly cultural and economic nationalism. The cultural nationalists fear Canada's cultural absorption by the United States, and the economic nationalists seek to repatriate to Canada much that is foreign owned, primarily by the United States.

Some Canadians believe they will be Americanized or homogenized to U.S. attitudes, values, and identity through its books, magazines, films, radio, and television fare, which dominate the Canadian leisure agenda. This perception of cultural imperialism is strengthened by the physical size, proximity, power, and ownership in Canada of its neighbor to the south.

Since more than 70 percent of Canada's almost twenty-six million residents live within one hundred miles of the border--within easy reach of U.S. television signals--the seriousness with which both the Canadian television industry and the cultural and economic nationalists view the incursions by the U.S. stations is understandable.

Penetration by foreign media, mainly from the United States, is dramatic. In 1976, books not authored by Canadians formed 83 percent of book sales in Canada, and 96 percent of the films in Canadian theaters were foreign.[13] In 1973, just 2 percent of all recordings sold in Canada were produced by Canadian firms.[14] In television viewing, most Canadians simply prefer to watch U.S. television entertainment fare. In 1983, the Canadian Communication Department reported that in peak evening hours on English-language television, foreign programs accounted for a "startling" 85 percent of viewing, and overall, watching foreign shows comprised 77 percent of total viewing throughout the day.[15] There is simply little Canadian-produced drama to air: only 5 percent of all drama shows available in Canada in 1983 were Canadian produced.[16] (The percentage is higher, however, for Canadian news, public affairs, and information shows).

By the mid-1980's, despite pay television, satellites, satellite dishes, VCRs and special funding arrangements to encourage Canadian productions, such as Telefilm, the problems continued, according to a major report recommending changes in the Broadcast Act. The task force found that by 1986, 98 percent of all drama on English television was foreign, while 90 percent of all drama on French television was foreign. Only 28 percent of all programming available on English television was Canadian. For younger Canadians, the picture was not much better. Francophone teenagers spent more than half their viewing time watching foreign programs; Anglophone teenagers spent 80 percent of their viewing time watching foreign programs.[17]

Foreign ownership is also dramatic. In 1978, the United States controlled 35.3 percent of manufacturing in Canada. In many key economic sectors, the United States share was even higher: in oil and gas, 47.1 percent; in rubber, 71.6 percent; in transportation and equipment, 69.2 percent; in chemicals, 52.9 percent; in electric equipment, 55.9 percent; in heavy machinery, 50.4 percent; and in textiles, 47.2 percent.[18] Although U.S. ownership in Canadian newspapers, radio, and television is negligible (largely restricted by Canadian legislation), significant ownership exists in publishing, cable, and recording industries. In 1976, 71 percent of the publishing industry was foreign controlled. In 1967, U.S. companies owned or controlled 77 percent of all Canadian cable subscribers, but that figure significantly decreased following passage of the 1968 Broadcasting Act. A number of cable companies were repatriated.[19]

A second root of the dispute lies in the apparently changing political relationship between the United States and Canada, at least from the 1960's to the election of Conservatives and Brian Mulroney in 1984. Canada, in those two decades, had grown more nationalistic, more desirous of charting its own course, and less accommodating to the will of the United States. There was a fear that through economic and media incursions, the United States would achieve de facto political control. The United States, meanwhile, responded with what Canadian political economist Stephen Clarkson called a policy of reciprocity, under which the United States answers with similar, and often retaliatory measures.[20] The United States, until 1984, at least, no longer appeared to have a special relationship with Canada, but rather treated Canada like any foreign country. If anything, Clarkson suggests, the United States expected Canada to be more exemplary in following the United States's developing codes on global investment and trade policy, which apply to all its international partners.

In the United States, under President Jimmy Carter, what Clarkson terms a "new doctrine of protectionism" evolved. Evidence includes amendments to the U.S. Trade Act of 1974. The border broadcasters were successful in having Congress add a key amendment to the Trade Act to make clear that the measure covered broadcasting, and that a complaint could be successfully pursued.

A third reason for the dispute lies in the aims and tortuous evolution of broadcasting in Canada. These include: (1) a private and public mix that in recent years has tipped to the private sector; (2) the tremendous growth of cable in Canada, which promotes U.S. over Canadian entertainment fare, and (3) the broadcasting statute itself, which requires attention to cultural content and identity aims. There was no restriction on the amount of foreign ownership in broadcasting prior to 1958, but concern over whether private broadcasting would be nationalized under a public broadcasting system effectively discouraged American interests from financial investment. In 1958, and again in 1968, Canada enacted broadcasting statutes, significantly reducing potential foreign ownership in radio and television. In 1969, Canada began to regulate the percentage of foreign-produced programming that could be aired. Canada has contended that since the stations south of the border do not need to meet the Canadian content requirements for programming, they are basically poachers without a license to service Canada.

The fourth root of the dispute is the Canadian perception that the vast media spillover--a modern Trojan horse--is causing a decline in Canadian culture and identity. Whether or not this view is fully supported, the Canadian perception of a dramatic effect is real and has encouraged passage of protective legislation. This perspective is illustrated by A. W. Johnson, former president of the Canadian Broadcasting Corporation, who stated, "We are in a fight for our soul, for our cultural heritage and for our nationhood. Without a culture, there is no political survival and we are not a nation."[21]

NOTES

1. Canadian Foreign Policy Texts, External Affairs Canada, Domestic Information Programs Division, April 1982, p. 1. The figure here was in 1980.

2. Ibid. p. 2.

3. The three in Buffalo are WIVB (formerly WBEN), WGR, and WKBW. The station in Bellingham is KVOS. These were the major stations involved in the dispute, as they received the bulk of the Canadian advertising revenue. Additional stations have been involved in the dispute at various times. The twenty-four station figure is derived from stations signing legal documents in the late 1970's (see Table 1). Leslie G. Arries, Jr., president of WIVB, Buffalo, testified in 1986 that sixty stations along the border felt the loss (see "Broadcasters seek resolution of trade dispute with Canada," Broadcasting, October 6, 1986, p. 60).

4. The $20 million for the gross Canadian revenue is used throughout most of the documents in the border dispute--reports of Canadian and U.S. governmental meetings, Canadian agency reports, border station materials, news media accounts, and legal records. It is an estimate, however, that varies by year, by how many border stations are involved at that point in the dispute, and by who is doing the survey. In addition, about 25 percent of the gross remained in Canada (15 percent to Canadian advertising agencies and 10 percent to Canadian sales representatives).

5. Rogers Cable Television Co. in Toronto, Coaxial Colourview Limited and Bramalea Telecable. CRTC decision 74-100, 74-101, and 74-102 (1972).

6. Jack Miller, "Buffalo-TV Stations Threaten to Blackout Canada." Toronto Star, 6 February 1975, p. 1.

7. Capital Cities Communication Inc. et al. v. Canadian Radio-Television Commission (1974), 52 D. L. R. 3d 415.

8. Section 3 of Bill C-58 (1st Session, Thirteenth Parliament, 23-24 Elizabeth II, 1974-75) was proclaimed law on September 22, 1976, and became Section 19.1 of the Income Tax Act. Bill C-58 was more widely known as a Canadian attempt to blunt Time and Reader's Digest from overwhelming the Canadian magazine market, by making advertising in foreign magazines nondeductible.

9. Proposed Foreign Conventions Amendment, prepared in 1977 by counsel to U.S. border stations, for U.S. senators. Also, House of Representatives report no. 95-1684, 95th Congress, 2nd Session, October, 1978, p. 2.

10. Canadian Office of Tourism press release, issued in February 1977, p. 1.

11. Federal Register, vol. 45, no. 150, August 1, 1980, p. S1173-4.

12. Bureau of National Affairs, "Taxation and Accounting," no. 178, September 11, 1980, p. 9.

13. Abraham Rotstein, "Canada: The New Nationalism", Foreign Affairs, vol. 55 (October 1976):11.

14. S. M. Crean, Who's Afraid of Canadian Culture? (Don Mills, Ontario: General Publishing Co., 1976), p. 17.

15. Francis Fox, Canadian Minister of Communications, Towards a New National Broadcast Policy. (Ottawa: Minister of Supply and Services, Canada, 1983). Document undated other than 1983 but made public in March, p. 8.

16. Ibid.

17. Gerald Lewis Caplan and Florian Sauvageau, co-chairmen, Report of the Task Force on Broadcasting Policy, Minister of Supply Services, Canada, 1986, p. 691.

18. Canadian Foreign Policy Texts, p. 4.

19. Some $125 million in Canadian broadcasting was returned to Canadian ownership by 1971. See Robert E. Miller, "The CRTC: Guardian of the Canadian Identity," Journal of Broadcasting, 172 (Spring 1973):194.

20. Stephen Clarkson, Canada and the Reagan: Crisis in the Canadian-American Relationship. (Toronto: James Lorimer Co., 1982), p. 236.

21. A. W. Johnson, president of the Canadian Broadcasting Corporation, in a statement entitled "Touchstone for the CBC," June 1977, p. 5.

Part II
Advertising Controls

2
Deletion Days

Initial skirmishes in the television border dispute began in the late 1960's, as concern mounted over the practice of Canadian stations airing U.S. programs and films before the U.S. stations did. The U.S. border stations contended the prerelease of network programming gave the Canadian stations an unfair advantage for viewers and advertisers.[1] The full-scale battles, however, did not begin until Canada enacted two measures in the 1970's to retain media advertising: (1) The CRTC-mandated random deletion by Canadian cable companies of American commercials from programs transmitted by U.S. border stations; (2) tax legislation (Bill C-58) making it more advantageous for a Canadian company seeking to reach the Canadian market to advertise on Canadian stations rather than on television stations south of the border.

The two measures are viewed in this study as an expression of economic nationalism, rationalized as necessary to enhance the cultural and identity objectives formulated in the Broadcasting Act of 1968. The U.S. border stations saw the measures as costing them millions: the average gross Canadian revenue earned for six of the U.S. border stations during the 1973-75 period was $17 million, of which more than 90 percent was garnered by the three network-affiliated stations in Buffalo, New York, and one in Bellingham, Washington.[2] The border stations mounted a massive campaign to retain the revenue for their stations, and legal counsel in both Ottawa and Washington, D.C., were hired to lobby, in some instances to sue and litigate, and generally monitor the ebb and flow of what the news media described as the "border war."[3]

Commercial deletion, and then Bill C-58, set off a chain of events that didn't wind down until 1988. This section and the next narrate the events and issues in that chain, from the start of commercial deletion in 1971, through the passage and impasse of Bill C-58, enacted in 1976. The dominant theme of this five-year period is the economics of broadcasting: the advertising dollar and the efforts by both sides to keep it for themselves.

THE STAKES

During the years 1973, 1974, and 1975, six of the U.S. border stations, including three in Buffalo, shared $15 to $18 million in gross Canadian advertising revenue, according to a summary prepared for the stations by Price Waterhouse & Co. The stations--KVOS in Bellingham; WBEN, WGR, and WKBW, all of Buffalo--reported the following gross Canadian revenue during the three-year period: $15.4 million in 1973, on total broadcast revenue of $40.5 million; $17.2 million in 1974, on a total of $42.8 million; and $18.4 million in 1975, on a total of $44.8 million (see Tables 2 and 3). Gross Canadian revenue for these six border stations comprised 39 percent of all their revenue in 1973; 40 percent in 1974, and 41 percent in 1975.

The figure for the gross Canadian revenue used throughout most of the documents in the border dispute--Canadian and U.S. governmental sessions and meetings, Canadian agency reports, border station materials, news media accounts, legal records--is $20 million. It is an estimate, however, that varies by year, number of border stations involved, and who is doing the survey. Tables 2 and 3 depict the gross advertising for six border stations in 1975, as compiled by Price Waterhouse & Co., was $18.4 million. Price Waterhouse & Co. subsequently compiled a survey of ten border stations, which indicates a 1975 figure of $18.9 million. The U.S. Federal Communications Commission (FCC) surveyed essentially the same stations as the latter study by Price Waterhouse & Co. and found a gross Canadian revenue of $18 million, but for 1974. A Toronto research firm, Donner and Lazar, hired as a consultant by the Canadian Department of Communication, placed the figure at $21 million for 1975.[4] (See Table 4 depicting the variety of estimates.)

For purposes of this study, the $20 million figure is used, but with clarifications. The first is that of the $20 million, about 25 percent remained in Canada: 15 percent went to advertising agencies and 10 percent went to sales representatives.[5] As Table 3 depicts, for example, more than $4 million of the $17 million earned by the six border stations in 1974 stayed in Canada through advertising expenses.

TABLE 2

CANADIAN ADVERTISING REVENUE FOR SIX U.S. TELEVISION BORDER STATIONS IN 1973-75, PROJECTED FOR 1978

Total Canadian advertising revenue	$15,408,903	$17,198,651	$18,393,044	$20,463,415
Amounts remaining in Canada: agency commissions	$ 2,200,572	$ 2,475,781	$ 2,601,714	$ 2,882,719
Sale representative commission	$ 942,539	$ 1,013,023	$ 1,004,816	$ 1,070,547
Other	$ 663,109	$ 867,863	$ 1,025,199	$ 1,255,000
Amount net of commissions, received from Canadian advertisers to reach U.S. audience only*	$ 2,253,887	$ 2,849,810	$ 2,883,203	$ 3,315,532

*Two of the six television stations were unable to provide the requested information for each of the periods presented.

The amounts were obtained from the following six stations, all of which reported information for each of the years presented, except as noted above: WBEN-TV, Buffalo, NY; WGR-TV, Buffalo, NY; WKBW-TV, Buffalo, NY; KVOS-TV, Bellingham, WA; WPTZ-TV, North Pole, NY; and WWNY-TV, Watertown, NY.

Source: Price Waterhouse & Co., July 29, 1976.

TABLE 3

TOTAL BROADCAST REVENUE FOR SIX U.S. TELEVISION BORDER STATIONS

	YEARS ENDED DECEMBER 31		
	1973	1974	1975
Total broadcast revenue	$40,513,486	$42,801,550	$44,835,501
Commissions	6,932,508	7,355,596	7,321,241
Net broadcast revenue	33,580,978	35,445,954	37,514,260
Total broadcast expenses	22,380,490	22,304,401	23,867,298
Broadcast operating income	$12,200,488	$13,141,553	$13,646,962

The amounts were obtained from the following six stations, all of which reported information for each of the three years presented, except as noted above: WBEN-TV, Buffalo, NY; WGR-TV, Buffalo, NY; WKBW-TV, Buffalo, NY; KVOS-TV, Bellingham, WA; WPTZ-TV, North Pole, NY; and WWNY-TV, Watertown, NY.

Source: Price Waterhouse & Co., July 29, 1975.

TABLE 4

CANADIAN-PLACED ADVERTISING REVENUE ON U.S. BORDER TELEVISION STATIONS, ALTERNATIVE ESTIMATES, 1975-1978

	1975	1976	1977	1978
Total Canadian Revenue[1]	$18,885,088	$16,781,230		$ 9,175,251
Net Canadian Revenues	$14,052,665	$12,319,303	$ 6,133,273	
KVOS-TV Revenues[2]	$ 7,421,920	$ 6,542,454	$ 4,113,463	$ 3,153,000
KVOS-TV Net Revenues	$ 6,113,865	$ 5,629,881	$ 3,578,290	$ 2,174,000
Buffalo	$ 9,300,000[3]			$ 3,700,000[4]
Bellingham	$ 7,000,000			$ 3,500,000
Other	$ 4,700,000			$ 1,000,000
Total Canadian Revenues	$21,000,000			$ 8,200,000

Net revenues exclude agency commissions and sales representative commission paid in Canada.

[1]Price Waterhouse & Co.; Survey of Canadian Advertising Financial Data (ten reporting stations), February 3, 1978.
[2]Wotmeco Enterprises, Inc.; owners of KVOS; written information prepared for Donner and Lazar.
[3]Howard Turetsky; Faulkner, Dawkins & Sullivan, April 17, 1975.
[4]David Mulcaster, CRTC; estimates provided to the Canadian Department of Communication.

Source: Donner & Lazar Research Associates, The Impact of the 1976 Income Tax Amendment on United States and Canadian TV Broadcaster. January 1979, T-1.

The second clarification is that whatever precise gross figure is used, the bulk of Canadian advertising goes to television stations in Buffalo, and Bellingham, subsequently leaders in the campaign to resurrect the funding. The three network-affiliated Buffalo stations in 1974 derived $9 million in gross revenue from Canadian advertisers, which represented about 30 percent of the Buffalo stations' total advertising revenue, as Philip Beuth, then vice president and general manager of Buffalo's Channel 7, WKBW-TV, indicated in testimony before a Canadian House of Commons committee.[6]   The net Canadian revenue taken out of Canada by the three Buffalo stations was an estimated $6 million after advertising commissions remaining in Canada were deducted.[7]   KVOS-TV in Bellingham took $6.7 million out of Canada in gross advertising revenue in 1974, which represented about 90 percent of the station's revenue, according to testimony by David Mintz, then president of the station, before a Canadian House of Commons committee.[8]

The third clarification is that the $20 million estimate is based on all the gross Canadian revenue from U.S. stations from one end of the border to the other.   However, the bulk came from the aforementioned six stations, depicted in Table 2.

DELETION BEGINS

The stage was set for the television border dispute in July, 1971, when the CRTC issued a policy statement for cable television describing several methods "to reduce the economic impact" of the penetration of the U.S. television stations into Canada, therefore enhancing the capacity of the Canadian broadcasting system to achieve national broadcasting objectives.[9]   One of the methods proposed was that cable operators remove American commercials from U.S. programs, but retain the shows received from the American stations.[10]   As a condition for a cable license, cable operators were required by the CRTC to randomly delete the commercials on U.S. border stations' signals and replace them with public service announcements.   Initially, the CRTC had conceived of replacing the United States' commercials with Canadian ones but "retreated" from that position.[11]   The rationale for commercial deletion was that Canadian advertisers would be leary of running ads on the U.S. border stations if they did not know if the intended audience would receive them; it was hoped the advertisers would shift to Canadian stations, and the additional revenue be used to improve Canadian production.

The first application of the CRTC policy was in December, 1972, by a Calgary, Alberta, cable company seeking a CRTC license to receive signals from a station in Spokane, Washington. As a condition of the license, the commission required that the cable company delete the commercials from signals from Spokane. With this precedent, the

CRTC began to make mandatory the deletion of U.S. commercials by cable systems when a cable operator's license came up for renewal before the commission. Subsequent to the Calgary case, commercial deletion clauses were included as part of the license renewals of cable operators in Montreal, the Maritimes, British Columbia, and Edmonton.[12]

The first direct clash in the "war," however, did not commence until Rogers Cable Television Company of Toronto began to delete commercials from Buffalo's WKBW, Channel 7, in August, 1973. It was done on a random basis[13] and without prior amendment to its license by the CRTC. In October, 1973, Rogers Cable, together with Coaxial Colourview Ltd. and Bramalean Telecable, applied to the CRTC for amendments to their broadcast licenses to allow deletion of commercials and substitution of special promotional messages and general public interest announcements. However, no promotional material was to be substituted; instead, public service announcements were to serve as primary replacements in the CRTC authorization granted through a license amendment.[14] The CRTC move led to legal action in the Canadian courts by the Buffalo stations, against both the CRTC and Rogers. The case against the CRTC was ultimately to be decided by the Canadian supreme court.

COURT ACTION

In May of 1974, three Buffalo stations--WGR, Channel 2; WKBW, Channel 7; and WBEN, Channel 4--appealed the CRTC decisions in Canada's federal court of appeals.[15] Issues raised included the question of whether the federal or provincial governments had the constitutional right to regulate cable. The federal court of appeals ruled in January, 1975, in favor of the CRTC, saying cable operators have the right to delete commercials because the CRTC has the right to authorize the practice. The court said that the border stations are using Canadian air space, which is public property, and when public property is used, the border stations do not acquire any right, either in the frequency or the signals they generate on it. "And they have no right to have their signals received in Canada in any form, whether altered or unaltered," the court said.[16]

The Buffalo stations reacted on two fronts: they appealed the decision to the Canadian supreme court and threatened to jam their signals to Canada to black out American television to Canadians.

JAMMING WARNED

Within a month of the Canadian lower court's decision not to bar commercial deletion, the three Buffalo stations, which at the time were estimated to attract about 45 percent of Toronto area's television audience, made known they were considering jamming their signals to the north, in effect deleting their programs to Canadians.[17] One proposal involved the stations moving their individual transmitters to a common tower on Grand Island in the Niagara River and beaming their signals only south and east, with virtually no strength to the north. (The stations have separate towers twenty miles southwest of Buffalo, and their signals are beamed in a circular pattern, with equal power in all directions.) Leslie Arries, Jr., then vice president and general manager of Buffalo's WBEN (now WIVB), Channel 4, commented at the time:

> The [Canadian] cable companies bring in our signals to help themselves attract clients, swelling their own profits. If they think they can exploit our service that way for their own gain on the one hand and, on the other hand, take action that will cost us millions of dollars, they should know we are not going to sit still for it.[18]

Phil Lind, then vice president and secretary of Rogers Cable, responded that the Buffalo stations' plan would be no real deterrent to picking up American network signals:

> It would be 'a piece of cake' to pick up the signal by microwave from Niagara Falls. . . . It might cost a million dollars, but spread out the cost between all the cable companies and it would not run too much. In any case, we could pick up the signals from the three network stations in Rochester.[19]

The Buffalo stations asked the FCC for permission to cut their signals to Canada. The FCC advised the Buffalo stations that it would not be a violation of international law for them to jam their own signals to keep them from being picked up by cable television in Canada.[20] The three Buffalo stations had applied to the FCC for an experimental license to control their own coverage by breaking up their signals through white noise--random pulses sent over a frequency that can cause a television picture to deteriorate--or other devices before it reached the cable transmitters in Canada.

Raymond E. Spence, chief engineer of the FCC, responded:

> After our initial, horrified shock on receiving the application from the stations, we examined the law and discovered that we are able--and almost obliged--to grant the stations the right to keep their signals out of Canada, as long as there is no interference with Canadian frequencies.[21]

The FCC's preliminary decision was sent to Canada's Department of Communication for its input. The proposal was reported to have "upset" the Canadian government, which ordered an inquiry on whether such jamming was permissible under international law.[22]   The border stations also sent a letter of protest to sixteen members of the Canadian Commons Committee on Broadcasting, Films and Assistance to the Arts explaining the border stations' position, describing themselves as "helpless victims of an edict by the CRTC which we regard as immoral and illegal."[23]

PEACE TALKS

The Buffalo stations did not proceed with jamming as efforts mounted for intergovernmental diplomatic talks. The border stations applied to the U.S. secretary of state and the U.S. State Department for a meeting with officials from both countries, but the response was "disappointing," according to WKBW's Philip Beuth.[24] WBEN's Leslie G. Arries, Jr. explained the U.S. State Department has asked the Canadian government for an answer regarding formal talks, and the answer came back that the matter was in the Canadian courts and the Canadian government preferred not to meet until they made some resolution.[25]

Informal talks and efforts for a formal forum continued, however, and an initial government-to-government meeting was held January 13, 1976, in Ottawa. Its purpose was to discuss the range of border television issues, according to Robert J. McCloskey, assistant Secretary for congressional relations at the U.S. State Department.[26] McCloskey said the focus of the talks was on Canadian's commercial deletion policy, but Bill C-58 was also discussed since it was believed to be "an integral part" of the border television program. (The legislation was then under consideration in Canada's Parliament.) The meeting's result was that the Canadian government "agreed to consider alternative means [than deletion] of achieving its communication policy objectives," according to McCloskey.[27] That night, CFRB-Radio in Toronto reported an "apparent truce" in what the news media had been calling for some time the Canada-U.S. border television war.[28] Parliamentary correspondent Scott Evans said the Canadian officials agreed to look at ways other than commercial deletion to repatriate the advertising dollars spent on the border stations.

A week later, on January 21, 1976, A. R. O'Brien, counsel for the border stations in Ottawa, met with Ralph Hart, policy advisor at the CRTC, seeking "what the Commission had in mind by way of a dollar value" when reference was made "to alternative means for achieving the objectives of the Canadian broadcast system."[29] In a report to the border stations' counsel in Washington, O'Brien stated:

The case I put to Mr. Hart was simply this: given that the United States representatives propose on or before a subsequent meeting to present to Canada alternatives for achieving the objectives of securing to the Canadian broadcasting system dollars now otherwise spent on United States border systems, how much realistically of the total amount spent on all border stations or on Buffalo would the Canadian Radio-television Commission expect to flow back to the Canadian broadcasting system.

In summary, Mr. Hart politely declined to forecast any figure, except to observe that the Commission hoped that all monies now spent by Canadian advertisers on United States television to reach primarily the Canadian audience would be repatriated.[30]

The border stations' counsel in Ottawa speculated that some of the advertising dollars went beyond publicly cited objectives but were for Canadian firms--CITY-TV, an independent station in Toronto, and Global, a television company in the province of Ontario. O'Brien noted:

It seems to me that the objectives . . . are, in the minds of the commission, more than simply insuring that more dollars are directed to programming. One of the objectives as alluded to by Hart would be to assist the CITY-TV and Global achieving or reaching a state of financial stability.[31]

On March 18, 1976, nine U.S. television border stations proposed alternative means for achieving the objectives of the Canadian broadcasting system. The stations[32] listed two steps they were prepared to take if neither commercial deletion nor Bill C-58 were implemented:
1. Each station would establish a taxable presence in Canada to subject the station's income from Canadian advertisers to Canadian federal and provincial income tax, to the degree permitted by the laws of both Canada and the United States without double taxation.
2. As an additional expense of doing business, each U.S. border station, or its taxable Canadian unit, would pay annually as a business expense a portion of its net income from Canadian advertisers into a fund to be administered by the Canadian government or its designee. The purpose of the fund would be to strengthen the Canadian broadcast system (whether by extension of service, stimulation of Canadian programming production, or otherwise strengthening other Canadian creative and cultural resources relevant to broadcasting) provided that such payment is treated as currently deductible for purposes of any applicable U.S. or Canadian income tax.[33]

A BREAKTHROUGH

Although the broadcasters' proposal was not found acceptable, a breakthrough in this phase of the dispute appears to have been reached at a meeting of high-level Canadian and U.S. officials. Richard Vine, deputy assistant secretary of state, and FCC chairman Richard Wiley met with a Canadian team on October 6, 1976. The Canadian delegation included representatives of the Canadian secretary of state, external affairs, the Department of Communication, and the CRTC. However, according to a letter by Washington counsel for the border stations:

Harry Boyle [chairman of the CRTC] and Mike Shoemaker [director general] stayed home, reportedly on orders from the 'Office of the Prime Minister.' It is the State Department's view that this represented a downgrading of the CRTC and determination to handle at the Cabinet level . . . intelligence gleaned from a CRTC member is that Boyle was kept away on grounds that he would be unduly provocative.[34]

According to a letter by Kempton B. Jenkins, acting assistant secretary for congressional relations:

The United States side pressed the Canadian government to declare a moratorium on further implementation of its commercial deletion policy. We suggested that such a moratorium, perhaps for a period of three years, would allow time for consideration of alternative means of achieving Canadian broadcast objectives which would be less harmful to legitimate United States interest.

At the conclusion of that meeting, we were optimistic that a satisfactory accommodation of the deletion issue could be worked out.[35]

Jenkins added, "After consultation with the United States border stations, we have concluded, and have so informed the Canadian government, that the CRTC's decision provides for a satisfactory solution to the problem of border broadcasting for the present."[36]

Although the official communique released after the meeting noted only that officials met to discuss border television questions of mutual concern, it did not specify what they were. Rosenbloom indicated the talks did include Bill C-58.[37] The legislation had become law a month before this meeting.

Rosenbloom reported the United States's position presented at the session: "[commercial deletion] should be dropped or that, if

Canada would not eliminate the policy entirely, it should delay its implementation indefinitely and for a minimum of three years, to study the effects of Bill C-58 and other relevant factors."[38]

This moratorium was termed the "only compromise proposal" made by the U.S. team, according to the Rosenbloom report to the border stations.[39]   He indicated that it was not clear what would be done regarding stopping the deletions in Calgary and Rogers Cable in Toronto, but that new acts of deletion would be suspended for three years. His report stated:

> [The Canadian officials] indicated that the proposal [on deletion of commercials] would not necessarily require the immediate elimination of the formal conditions on Canadian cable licenses relating to commercial deletion, so long as no deletion goes on. There was a fuzzy understanding that existing situations would be left unaffected, i.e., that the deletion going on in Calgary (at the expense of the Spokane stations) would not have to be halted. The application of this exception to the Rogers systems in Toronto was left murky.

> It was made clear, however, that there could be no automatic assumption that commercial deletion would go forward at the end of the three year period. Instead, both sides would meet to discuss and evaluate the results.[40]

Rosenbloom reported the Canadian team did not have final authority to commit its side. They had, however, some alternatives that had not been fully cleared with their ministers but to which they wanted U.S. reactions. This included a proposal that both countries prohibit stations from selling time in the other country. Chairman Wiley of the FCC "immediately rejected" this as contrary to the U.S. regulatory and general philosophy of free competition, according to the Rosenbloom account.[41]

Rosenbloom concluded:

> At the press briefing, both sides stressed that progress was being made. Privately, the Canadian delegation indicated that they [sic] should have a report to Cabinet in about three weeks. There was no pressure from the United States side for quicker action--a deliberate choice--and no specific agreement that there must be another formal meeting. It is conceivable that things will be allowed to sit with no formal announcement for some time. In the meantime, there will be no further implementation of deletion.[42]

A headline the next day in the <u>Toronto Star</u> read "Border War Cools: End Hinted to United States Ad Cuts from Cable TV."[43]

The issues were subsequently discussed October 15, 1976, a little more than a week after the aforementioned meeting, at a U.S. State Department session between Henry Kissinger, secretary of state, and Donald Jamieson, Canadian external affairs minister. Jamieson was reported telling Kissinger that "he was optimistic a satisfactory accommodation could be worked out."[44]

The day after the Kissinger-Jamieson talks, October 16, 1976, the CRTC announced it was extending the deadline for the commission to be informed by cable operators on plans for deletion. The new date was August 31, 1977. The CRTC had made it a condition of a number of cable television licenses in various parts of Canada that plans for commercial deletion be developed by cable television licenses in conjunction with television broadcasters for the further implementation of commercial deletion, and that the commission be informed of the development by specified dates.[45]

The Cabinet of Canadian prime minister Pierre Trudeau decided on a moratorium on random deletion at its last meeting before Christmas, 1976, reported Geoffrey Stevens, a journalist for the Globe and Mail. Stevens said Jamieson wrote to Kissinger late in December to inform him of the Canadian cabinet decision, and to advise him that the moratorium will remain in effect until Ottawa has a chance to assess the impact of the broadcasting provisions of Bill C-58 on the advertising revenues of Canadian broadcasters. At the end of December, Stevens noted, the cabinet decision was conveyed to the CRTC. The cabinet could not order the CRTC to impose a moratorium, so its decision had to be "couched" as a request. The CRTC was not scheduled to act until late January, 1977.[46]

MORATORIUM ANNOUNCED

As 1977 began, random commercial deletion was being practiced in Calgary, Edmonton, and some parts of Toronto, but the CRTC announced on January 21, 1977, a moratorium on new deletion orders. The commission explained it had been informed by Jeanne Sauve, minister of communications, that the government fully supported the objectives leading to institute the commercial deletion policy, but considers that the feasibility of other methods of achieving the same objectives should be examined by the commission before further commercial deletion is implemented.[47] In addition, the government considered that time should be allowed for an assessment of the effect of Bill C-58 and of simultaneous program substitution.[48]

The CRTC said it welcomed government support for the objectives of its regulatory policies, and that the commission would undertake the requested examination and assessment. The CRTC noted that the period of assessment would also enable the commission to receive the judgment of the Canadian supreme court on the commission's jurisdiction with respect to commercial deletion, which continues to be authorized for implementation by several cable television licenses as a condition of their license.[49]

Rosenbloom questioned the timing of the CRTC announcement. It was speculated that the government withheld the announcement because of the expected decision in the Canadian supreme court on the Buffalo stations' appeal. The government, it was felt, feared that the announcement would weaken the federal case in court, or that the court would refuse to hear the Buffalo appeal on the grounds it was moot.[50]

Rosenbloom concurred in speculating that the CRTC and the Canadian government wanted the case in its supreme court to go forward. The CRTC, according to Rosenbloom, had been "afraid" that the moratorium might render the case too "iffy" and hypothetical, resulting in a dismissal or indefinite delay of judgment by the court. The CRTC and the government's argument now, Rosenbloom reasoned, is that the matter is not moot or "iffy" because Rogers, Calgary, and Edmonton cable operators were authorized to delete and were deleting.[51]

The three Buffalo stations, meanwhile, were seeking an out-of-court settlement with Rogers.[52] Rosenbloom, however, indicated it was not likely that the CRTC--which had ordered Rogers not to settle his private litigation with the Buffalo stations without its approval--would agree to a settlement until the Canadian supreme court had decided.[53]

Rosenbloom felt that the moratorium did take some of the "psychological steam" out of the CRTC's case in the supreme court. He added:

> While the case is not technically moot, the court must know that it is being asked to rule on a controversy that could very easily disappear shortly after it rules. The court may even get the impression that the controversy is being kept artificially alive for the sole purpose of obtaining its ruling (and it would, of course, be right). In these circumstances, while the odds are against use in the Supreme Court of Canada continue to be heavy . . . I would not expect a decision against us by the Supreme Court to affect the moratorium to which the Canadian government and the CRTC are fully committed.[54]

SUPREME COURT ACTS

The appeal to the supreme court was heard January 27, 28, and 29, 1977, by a full court.[55] Although the border stations were principally seeking decisions in areas of broadcast regulations--mainly whether the CRTC had the power to authorize a cable company to delete commercials from the American stations--the case included the constitutional appeal as well: whether cable television was subject exclusively to federal oversight or whether the provinces had jurisdiction. The question drew broad Canadian interest and debate. Four provinces--Ontario, Quebec, British Columbia, and Alberta-- intervened to support the Buffalo stations in their objection to the authority of the Parliament over cable distribution, according to a report to the border stations' Washington counsel from one of the Ottawa barristers who argued the case before the Canadian supreme court.

The CRTC, Rogers, and the federal government argued for federal jurisdiction. The province of Saskatchewan supported divided jurisdiction, taking the position that a cable company works in a local area, but that the federal power could order that any given part of a signal emanating from the United States not be received in Canada.

The Canadian supreme court announced its decision on November 30, 1977, nearly ten months after the hearings: the CRTC had the power to authorize commercial deletion. The authority over cable was a federal, not a provincial, power.[56] In writing the six-to-three decision, Chief Justice Bora Laskin noted that while the Canadian Broadcasting Act provides the unquestioned right of persons to receive programs, that doesn't preclude the commission from authorizing cable television companies to delete commercial messages.[57]

On the constitutional issue, Laskin said the court couldn't accept the contention that signals are under federal jurisdiction until they reach the cable company's community antenna and then become the authority of the province in which the antenna is located.[58] Laskin noted:

> Federal legislative authority extends to the regulation of the reception of television signals emanating from a source outside of Canada and to the regulation of the transmission of such signals within Canada. Those signals carry the programs which are ultimately viewed on home television sets; and it would be incongruous, indeed, to admit federal legislative jurisdiction to the extent conceded but to deny the continuation of the regulatory authority because the signals are intercepted and sent on to ultimate viewers through a different technology (from over-the-air to cable).[59]

There were three additional questions before the Supreme Court. One was whether international conventions (the Inter-American Radio Communication convention of 1937) prohibiting interference with signals and retransmissions were violated. The majority of the court answered no.[60] A second question, in two parts, was whether the CRTC exceeded its jurisdiction by requiring any private settlement by Rogers and the Buffalo stations to be approved by the CRTC, and whether the CRTC exceeded its jurisdiction because commercial deletion was passed on a policy statement rather than a law or regulation. The court ruled a private settlement between Rogers and the Buffalo stations did not need the consent of the CRTC and that a decision based on only a policy statement was proper.[61] The final question was whether the Buffalo stations had standing, or status, to pursue litigation. The latter question was raised in terms that invited the court to determine what, if any, were the proprietary rights of the Buffalo stations signals upon their entry into Canadian air space. The question didn't arise for an answer, the court stated, and thus the question was not answered by the high court.[62]

REACTION TO DELETION

Although there was some support in some quarters in Canada for commercial deletion, there was strong and widespread opposition. "Piracy" and "unethical" were frequently seen in headlines. An editorial in the Globe and Mail[63] termed deletions "shabby, sleazy, shoddy, immoral, dishonest, beneath contempt--but not beneath the CRTC." Opposition was joined by the Toronto Star, the Winnipeg Free Press and the Toronto Sun. Peter Worthington, executive editor of the Sun, in personal correspondence, condemned deletion.[64] Chambers of commerce, cable companies (including systems in British Columbia, the Yukon and Ontario), as well as the private Canadian television network decried the deletion policy. John T. Coleman, director for government and industry liaison for the CTV Television Network, Ltd. in Toronto, noted in personal communication that the CTV's corporate position was one of opposition.[65]

On the other hand, Moses Znaimer, president of CITY-TV, the independent station in Toronto, stated that allegations of stealing, and unethical and immoral conduct were a "lot of nonsense." "[American broadcasters] steal into a market for which they have no license and sell a commodity they haven't bought. For them to pretend that they are the morally outraged party is the grossest kind of hypocrisy."[66]

In the United States, WKBW's Philip Beuth responded: "We look at this [commercial deletions] as a maneuver by the CRTC to have it both ways: to keep United States programs for which cable operators pay not one penny while blocking our chance to earn any compensation. This is a concept to which we object strenuously."[67]

Jack Lester, general manager of two television stations in North Fargo, North Dakota, WDAY and WDAZ, in personal communication, concurred with Beuth. Lester assailed deletion as a "rip-off" and "an act of international piracy."[68]

The border stations were also gaining support in Congress. U.S. Representative John J. LaFalce, whose constituency includes the Buffalo area, commented in personal correspondence that the three network affiliates in Buffalo were "absolutely correct--the deletion of commercials was . . . an act of pure piracy." LaFalce added he was prepared "to help secure" approval for the jamming "should it have become necessary."[69]   Additional support was being generated not only in the House, but in the Senate, White House,and among high-level governmental agencies, as will be depicted in the next chapter.

NOTES

1. Prerelease becomes a problem for the border stations when the signals of Canadian stations enter U.S. markets either via cable or off the air. Residents of the Buffalo area, for example, can often watch American network films on Canada's Channel 5 (CBC) or 9 (CTV) before they are shown on affiliate stations in Buffalo. In December of 1969, WBEN (Channel 4 in Buffalo, a CBS affiliate) went before the Federal Communications Commission seeking to curb the prerelease practice of CBS. WBEN argued that since it was in direct competition for viewers and advertisers with Canadian television stations, the Canadian stations had an unfair advantage by the prerelease policy the FCC had approved for CBS. At issue were eighteen prime time CBS network programs being released on Canadian stations prior to the time they are made available to U.S. stations. ABC and NBC also prereleased shows in Canada. Additional legal action was pursued through the first half of the 1970's.

2. The $17 million in Canadian revenue is an average for the three-year period 1973, 1974, and 1975 (of $15.4 million, $17.2, million and $18.4 million, respectively), derived from data provided by the stations to Price Waterhouse & Co. in 1976 by six border stations.

3. Counsel for the border stations during this period in Washington included Fletcher, Heald, Rowell, Kenehan, and Hildreth; Cordon and Jacobin; Wilmer, Cutter, and Pickering. Counsel in Ottawa included Hewitt, Hewitt, Nesbitt, Reid; Gowling and Henderson.

4. Arthur Donner and Fred Lazar, The Impact of the 1976 Income Tax Amendment on United States and Canada TV Broadcasters, January 1979, p. T-1.

5. Leslie Arries, Jr., then general manager, WBEN, Buffalo, in Minutes of Proceeding and Evidence of the Standing Committee on Broadcasting, Films and Assistance to the Arts, Canadian House of Commons, no. 29, December 1, 1975, p. 19.

6. Philip Beuth, then vice president and general manager, WKBW, Buffalo, in Minutes of Proceedings and Evidence of the Standing Committee on Broadcasting, Films and Assistance to the Arts, Canadian House of Commons, no. 29, December 1, 1975, p. 9.

7. In a data sheet to Price Waterhouse Co., one Buffalo station, WIVB, Channel 2 (formerly WBEN), reported for 1975 a total gross Canadian advertising revenue of $2.7 million, of which nearly $600,000 remained in Canada through Canadian advertising agency and sales commissions. Net Canadian revenues for WIVB (WBEN) would be $2.1 million and, since the three Buffalo network-affiliated stations have a similar share of the Canadian market and need to be competitive in advertising rates, the estimated net revenue for the Buffalo stations would be three times WIVB's, or $6.3 million.

8.   David Mintz, then president of KVOS, Bellingham, in <u>Minutes of Proceedings and Evidence</u> of the Standing Committee on Broadcasting, Films and Assistance to the Arts, Canadian House of Commons, no. 29, December 1, 1975, p. 9.

9.   Guy Lafebvre, secretary general, "Public Announcement: Commercial Deletion," CRTC annual report, January 21, 1971.

10.   The second was that cable operators black out both the programs as well as the advertisements in shows from U.S. television stations and simultaneously substitute the U.S. program from Canadian stations.   The process--simultaneous substitution--would allow for Canadian ads placed amid the American shows.   The simultaneous program substitution, which did not go into effect until April 1976, was in response to complaints by domestic broadcasters that they were losing audiences and advertising revenues because of the growing number of U.S. channels made available to Canadian viewers by cable.   The measure, unlike commercial deletion, drew some support from the border stations (see C. Gaylord Watkins, border stations' counsel, "Memorandum: Canada-United   States   Relations--Trans-border Broadcasting and Program Services," August 1978).   However, in latter stages in the dispute in the mid-1980s, the border stations opposed substitution as revenue losses to the border stations mounted.

11.   C. Gaylord Watkins, "Memorandum: Canada-United States Relations-- Trans-border Broadcasting and Program Services."   Prepared by Watkins, associate of Hewitt, Hewitt, Nesbitt, Reid, barristers and solicitors, Ottawa, for the border stations.   August 1978, p. 52.

12.   Donner and Lazar, p. I-1.

13.   Random basis, according to a telex message from Rogers, means three or more substitutions per evening on at least one of the channels on an alternate basis.   Rogers originally planned to substitute promotional messages to subscribers, such as free antenna removal, discounts for prepayment, additional channel offerings, as well as messages of general public interest.   The CRTC ultimately accepted only the latter category.   Overall, roughly 10 percent of the prime time commercials were replaced under commercial deletion; the tactic forced the Spokane television station to close its Calgary sales office a few weeks after random deletion began.

14.   CRTC, Decisions 74-100; 74-101; 74-102, in 1972.

15.   The appeal was of CRTC decisions 74-100, 74-101 and 74-102, to the federal court of appeals under Section 28 of the Federal Court Act and Section 26 of the Broadcast Act.   Eight months after the first appeal, the Buffalo stations, on October 1, 1975 appealed additional CRTC decisions (74-412 to 75-425) that were similar to the CRTC decisions for which the border stations went to court on in the first instance.   These authorized certain Toronto and Hamilton area cable systems to implement a policy of commercial deletion and substitution.   The appeal was stayed to await the decision of the first supreme court case.

16.   "Court Upholds CRTC Authority," <u>Canadian News Facts</u>, 1975, p. 1332.

17.   Jack Miller, "Buffalo-TV Stations Threaten to Black Out Canada." <u>Toronto Star</u>, February 6, 1975, p. 1.

18.   Ibid.

19.   Lawrence O'Toole, "Rogers Cable Claims No Danger in Buffalo Plan to Cut Off Signals," <u>Toronto Star</u>, February 7, 1975, p. 35.

20.   Les Brown, "Buffalo TV Plans A 'Jam' to Canada," <u>New York Times</u>, November 18, 1975, p. 67.

21. Ibid.

22. Ibid.

23. Leslie Arries, Jr., then general manager of WBEN, Buffalo, prepared model for letter sent to the Standing Committee on Broadcasting, Films and Assistance to the Arts, Canadian House of Commons, 1975.

24. Minutes of Proceedings and Evidence of the Canadian Standing Committee on Broadcasting, Films, and Assistance to the Arts, no. 29, December 1, 1975, p. 37.

25. Ibid.

26. Robert J. McCloskey, assistant secretary for congressional relations, U.S. State Department. Letter to Senator Warren G. Magnuson, replying to Magnuson's letter to the secretary in which Magnuson urged the secretary to contact the Canadian government regarding border broadcast stations' issues, 1976, p. 1.

27. Ibid.

28. Monitor-Script, "Cable Deletion" fifty-five second spot on CFRB-Radio in Toronto, January 13, 1976.

29. A. R. O'Brien, counsel for the border stations in Ottawa, in report, 1976, p. 1.

30. Ibid., p. 2.

31. Ibid., p. 3.

32. The stations that subscribed to the plan were WBEN, WGR, and WKBW, all of Buffalo; KVOS, Bellingham; WICU and WSEE, both in Erie, Pennsylvania; WWNY, Watertown, New York; WPTZ, Plattsburgh, New York; and WCAX, Burlington, Vermont.

33. Proposal by United States border television stations. "The Canadian-United States Border Television Problem and Alternative Means for Achieving Objectives and the Canadian Broadcast System," March 18, 1976, pp. 3-4.

34. Joel Rosenbloom, attorney with Wilmer, Cutter and Pickering, Washington, D.C., border stations' counsel, in letter to Thomas S. Murphy, chairman of the board of Capital Cities Communications, Inc., summarizes the October 6 inter-government meeting on the border dispute, 1976, p. 2.

35. Kempton B. Jenkins, acting assistant secretary for congressional relations, U.S. State Department, in letter to U.S. Representative Henry J. Nowak, 37th District, 1977, p. 1.

36. Ibid., p. 2.

37. Joel Rosenbloom, attorney of the firm of Wilmer, Cutter and Pickering, Washington, D.C., in a 1976 letter to Thomas S. Murphy, chairman of the board of Capital Cities Communication, p. 2. Capital Cities owned WKBW, Buffalo, New York.

38. Ibid.

39. Ibid., p. 3.

40. Ibid.

41. Ibid., p. 4.

42. Ibid., pp. 6-7.

43. Jack Miller, "Border War Cools: End Hinted to United States Ad Cuts from Cable TV," Toronto Star, October 7, 1976, p. A7.

44. Roland Powell, "United States Optimistic in Canadian Talks on Deletion of TV Commercials," Buffalo Evening News, November 24, 1976, p. 55.

45. CRTC Annual Report, p. 1.

46. Stevens, Geoffrey, "Cabinet OKs Moratorium," Globe and Mail, January 1, 1977, p. 6.

47. CRTC, p. 2.

48. Simultaneous substitution was enacted by the CRTC as a regulation that requested cable operators, when asked by Canadian television stations, to substitute the Canadian station's signals for the U.S. station's signals when the same program is being shown at the same time by both stations. The result for the viewers is that the Canadian broadcast and commercials are seen on both channels. Simultaneous substitution was seen, at the time, as less offensive to U.S. stations, since it does not involve appropriation of border stations' programming.

49. CRTC.

50. Rosenbloom, 1977 letter, p. 2.

51. Ibid.

52. Amended interim agreement and final agreement were sought by Buffalo stations--Capital Cities, owner of WKBW (Channel 7); Taft Broadcasting Co., owner of WGR (Channel 2); and owners of WBEN, from Rogers Cable, owner and operator of a cable television system in metropolitan Toronto, and Edward S. Rogers, chief executive officer, chairman of the board, and controlling stockholder in Rogers Cable, in Cap Cities et al. v. Rogers, March 29, 1977.

53. Rosenbloom.

54. Ibid.

55. The case had been scheduled for November 25, 1976, but then one of the nine judges fell ill and Chief Justice Bora Laskin put it off, saying this was a major constitutional matter and should be heard by the entire panel.

56. Capital Cities Communications, Inc. et al. v. Canadian Radio-Television Commission et al., 81 D.L.R. 3d 609. November 30, 1977.

57. Ibid., p. 610.

58. Ibid., p. 621.

59. Ibid., p. 623.

60. Ibid., pp. 630-633.

61. Ibid., pp. 628-630.

62. Ibid., p. 616.

63. "Thieving," an editorial, Globe and Mail, September 26, 1975, p. 15.

64. Peter Worthington, executive editor, the Toronto Sun. Letter relating his position on the border dispute, to Associate Professor Mary B. Cassata, State University of New York at Buffalo, May 16, 1975.

65. John T. Coleman, director, government and industry liaison CTV Television Network, Ltd., Toronto. Letter to Associate Professor Mary B. Cassata and Emanuel Levy, relating Coleman's position on the border dispute, May 5, 1977.

66. Moses Znaimer, president, CITY-TV, Toronto, "The Border Battle Intensifies Despite Bill C-58," Globe and Mail, November 5, 1875, p. 6.

67. Philip R. Beuth, vice president and general manager of WKBW, "Canada Stance is Called Discriminatory," Buffalo Courier-Express, February 29, 1976, p. 9.

68. Jack Lester, general manager, WDAY-TV (Ch. 6) and WDAZ-TV (Ch. 8), Fargo, North Dakota. Letter relating his position on dispute, to Associate Professor Mary B. Cassata, State University of New York at Buffalo, June 8, 1977.

69. John LaFalce,   United States Representative,   36th District. Letter relating his position on border dispute to Associate Professor Mary B. Cassata, State University of New York at Buffalo, June 6, 1977.

3
Legislation

Canadian efforts at retaining broadcast advertising revenue through an income tax measure were underway at the same time as the commercial deletion policy. Deletion was implemented much sooner, however, as it involved a CRTC rule and Bill C-58 required legislation by Parliament, a process that took about five years from concept to passage in 1976.

BILL C-58 GAINS SUPPORT

The first step was in 1971 when the CRTC recommended to the government that the provisions of the Income Tax Act should be amended "in order to offset the heavy financial involvement of United States border stations in the Canadian broadcast system."[1] The broadcasters subsequently were to press for implementation.

In 1973, the Canadian Association of Broadcasters (CAB), an organization then representing 388 broadcasting member stations, or about 90 percent of Canada's privately owned stations, initiated correspondence and discussions with various Cabinet ministers and their staffs on the question of Canadian advertising sold on U.S. border stations and beamed back at Canadian audiences. On October 31, 1974, the CAB, together with the Canadian Cable Television Association (CCTA), presented a brief to the federal government. J. Hugh Faulkner, then minister of state, introduced what was to become Bill C-58 on January 23, 1975. The House of Commons Standing Committee on Broadcasting, Films and Assistance to the Arts began hearings to amend the Income Tax Act of Canada, Section 19. Initially, the measure was primarily designed to reduce the advertising dominance of American periodicals in Canada, principally Time and Newsweek. The pair were overwhelming the Canadian market both in advertising lineage and circulation.[2]   Broadcasting controls were subsequently added to Bill C-58 as Section 3.   The bill would disallow income tax deductions for Canadian companies who advertise on the U.S. television border stations to reach the Canadian market.   Since corporate income tax in Canada is about 48 percent, Bill C-58 would make it twice as expensive to purchase air time on the border stations.

December 1975 was a busy month for Bill C-58.   The standing committee held hearings on the bill.   Officials from the Buffalo stations and the station in Bellingham attended as witnesses.   The CAB filled its brief with the committee outlining why the bill should be passed.   And Harry Boyle, chairman of the CRTC, was speaking out--against the border stations and for the bill.

The CAB contended the bill was needed to repair past inequities Canadian broadcasters faced in competing with the U.S. border stations.[3] Deploying a metaphor that was subsequently read into the Canadian senate debates on the bill, the CAB asserted: "What started as a 'soft spot' in the underbelly of Canadian broadcasting turned into a commercial tumor, and has been transformed into an economic cancer."[4]

The "soft spot" refers to the CAB position that, because of the Canadian lag in licensing broadcasting stations during the 1950's, television stations licensed in the United States were allocated lower frequency channels, which gave its border stations "strong, almost insurmountable economic advantages" over Canadian stations licensed later, and with higher, less desirable channel allocation.[5] The CAB also contended that although some U.S. stations were located in urban centers with a significant advertising base (but with signals strong enough to penetrate adjacent border areas; Buffalo, for example, has signals strong enough not only to serve its own market but adjacent Canadian areas as Hamilton-Toronto and the Golden Horseshoe), other U.S. border stations were licensed, according to the CAB, apparently to prey on the Canadian market since Washington, KVOS in Bellingham for example, has little advertising base of its own.

The border stations' advantage turned into a tumor and cancer, because, the broadcasters' organization claimed, the "competitive gap" continued to widen as the U.S. stations do not have the same economic requirements as Canadian stations, which carry high-cost Canadian content and are liable to the regulations of the CRTC and the objectives of the Broadcasting Act of 1968.[6] Thus, the CAB alleged:

> The United States stations are able to sell more competitively in Canada because they are able to purchase their products [programs] without taking into account their Canadian market and have no responsibility under the Broadcasting Act to internally cross-subsidize the development of

Canadian content programs as required by the CRTC and the regulations under the Broadcasting Act.[7]

The CAB argued that C-58 would provide four key benefits to Canada: (1) increase quality Canadian programming by the infusion of fresh revenue; (2) ensure the financial viability of new Canadian television stations in a difficult financial period; (3) provide new Canadian broadcasting jobs and strengthen the entire system; and (4) increase creative opportunities for Canadian performers, writers, producers, and technicians.[8]

FUNDS DRAINED

Many of the specific allegations against the border stations were presented in a speech, "Survival," by Boyle to the Men's Canadian Club of London, Ontario. Boyle charged that: (1) since 1950, more than $250 million had been extracted from Canada by the U.S. border stations; (2) more than $35 million is paid annually to American producers for programs shown in Canada; (3) border stations not licensed for Canada extract some $20 million a year in direct sales, or 10 percent of the television advertising revenue, in Canada in 1974; (4) multinational companies, recognizing the free spillover effect into Canada, and especially by way of cable systems carrying American programs into areas out of reach of border stations directly, can forego advertising in Canada in an amount estimated to be $30 to $40 million; and (5) border stations are slashing, or dumping, their advertising rate.[9]

Philip Beuth, of WKBW, apparently making a statement for the three Buffalo stations, said in testimony before the Standing Committee of the House of Commons Broadcasting, Films and Assistance to the Arts, that there was no basis for the claim that Buffalo stations have taken $250 million out of the Canadian market over the years. Beuth did not proffer a figure but did invite the committee to examine the stations' Canadian sales records.[10] During subsequent hearings in the Canadian senate, Senator Keith Davey recounted that he asked the Buffalo stations the total amount of their advertising sales in Canada since their inception. "There was a good deal of discussion back and forth about what I meant. I suggested it would be $100 million. I still regard that as a conservative estimate. The Buffalo stations said they thought it was not that high."[11]

Beuth, before the House of Commons Committee, denied that the Buffalo stations were dumping advertising in Canada (that is, that the Buffalo stations were not charging Canadian advertisers less for air time than American advertisers). He warned that Bill C-58 would squeeze out the small- and medium-sized advertiser in the Toronto market since that market, unlike the United States generally, is largely sold out in advance.[12]

Beuth also contended that if the border stations were cut out of the Toronto advertising market, the price of a spot by the remaining stations in Toronto would be substantially increased. "It is grossly overstated that the drain of Canadian revenue from Toronto stations put the Toronto stations in jeopardy."[13] Beuth contended the real problem the Buffalo stations cause is an audience problem: 45 percent of the metro Toronto market watches the Buffalo stations. Whether the Canadian ads remain on the border stations, Canadians will still be watching the Buffalo stations, Beuth asserted.

Beuth contended that the spillover effect is "grossly overstated and much misunderstood" and indicated the border stations would help finance the cost of an impartial study to determine how much multinational companies in the United States and Canada are not spending on Canadian stations.[14] The assumption is that the major multinationals were advertising on border stations, covering both north and south of the border, and therefore didn't need to advertise as much in Canada directly. The disagreement has been in the amount of loss to Canada due to this spillover. Figures have been cited of $30 million, $45 million, $100 million, $200 million, and $250 million annually.   Beuth testified at the broadcasting committee hearing that there is no demonstrated basis for a spillover claim of $200 million.[15]

It is also not true that Buffalo stations' suppliers are not paid extra for the additional Canadian market, according to Beuth.[16] The Buffalo stations pay extra for the non-network shows because of the additional Canadian audience.[17] Earl Beall, then general manager of WGR, explained that Taft Broadcasting, the owners of WGR in Buffalo, also own stations in two larger markets, and yet, for the Dinah Shore Show, WGR pays 50 percent more than does Buffalo's two sister stations in larger U.S. markets because of the Canadian audience.   For network shows, however, Beuth indicated that additional monies were not involved for the extra Canadian market because when the border stations' networks negotiate with program suppliers, the dollar amounts are so large that the Canadian viewership of the border affiliates is not a significant enough factor to have a substantial bearing on the negotiated price.[18]

Beuth indicated that the border stations would "like to sit down and talk at an appropriate forum" on ways to pay by taxation or otherwise, in one lump sum.[19] Until then, Beuth asked that the proposed bill be postponed.[20] If the bill were to be passed, Beuth added that the tax should be implemented over a period of five years.

The witnesses at the hearings by the standing committee depicted key differences between the major border broadcasters in the dispute: KVOS of Bellingham, and the three national-affiliated stations in Buffalo. KVOS, although its transmitter is in the United States and its signal is licensed by the FCC, has a primary Canadian market while the Buffalo stations' market is mainly western New York state.   KVOS drew 90 percent of its total 1974 revenue from

Vancouver-Victoria in British Columbia, and the Buffalo stations drew 30 percent from the Toronto-southern Ontario market.[21]

David Mintz, president of KVOS in British Columbia, explained his station was set up differently than Buffalo's. KVOS is a wholly owned Canadian subsidiary of KVOS on the American side of the border. It was incorporated as a Canadian company in 1955 and hires Canadian personnel. It built a film production company in western Canada and has contributed $75 million to Canada in taxes, reinvestments and payroll. Mintz proposed spending an additional $2 million in return for special consideration under Bill C-58.[22]

SENATE DEBATES BEGIN

After nine months of "most formidable opposition,"[23] the House of Commons passed Bill C-58 and the measure moved to the Canadian senate. Debates were held in the spring and summer of 1976. The Liberal Party's Senator Davey, the former chairman of the study by the Special Committee on Mass Media in 1971, was among the leading advocates of Bill C-58. First criticizing the CAB for a lack of contributions in the 1971 study--claiming the private broadcasters might be sophisticated individually but that as a group they "achieved a level perhaps best described as neanderthal"--Davey then praised the CAB under new leadership for beginning to move into the twentieth century.[24] He concurred with the CAB view that the border stations were an "economic cancer." Davey stated: "The three Buffalo stations derive 30 percent of their revenue from a market they were not licensed to serve, from a market served by Canadian stations playing under altogether different and more stringent ground rules."[25]

Senator Van Roggen noted what was to become an often-cited Canadian position, that Bill C-58 was an internal Canadian tax measure, and Canada's business entirely. He called for a treaty between Canada and the United States to work out the border broadcast difficulties.[26]

Senator Jacques Flynn, in opposing Bill C-58, warned, "We risk confrontation with the United States. . . . We would be telling our friends to the south, 'We will have what we want, or else.' "[27]

Davey, in subsequent debates of the senate, asked a rhetorical question: "Who it is that opposes the bill?" For openers, Davey answered:

There are all those American companies who, with their oh-so professional, highly skilled lobbyists, have a vested interest in the status quo. There are, for example, the American border television companies, who are understandably unhappy at the prospect of losing such a lucrative set-up.[28]

The senator referred to a commission session in which he was questioning the representatives from the Buffalo stations. Davey asked each how their stations, according to the objectives of the Broadcasting Act of 1968, enriches or strengthens the cultural, political, social, and economic fabric of Canada.[29] Only Philip Beuth is cited as replying. Beuth noted the Broadcasting Act also says that the right of all persons to receive signals should not be denied, but added, "those two sections of the Broadcasting Act are at odds with each other. I do not see any of that language as reason to take our product and deny us an opportunity to be compensated for it[commercial deletion]."[30]

At the same point, Beuth, before the House of Commons Standing Committee on Broadcasting, Films and Assistance to the Arts, had stated:

> Our contribution to Canada has been, first, providing a fair recompense for a valuable advertising vehicle for Toronto advertisers who have marketed their goods and services with it quite effectively, and, second, one of our contributions to Canada is the existence of a very profitable [Canadian] cable television industry.[31]

Davey also asked each representative of the Buffalo stations if, when Bill C-58 passes, whether the station will be forced out of business. All answered no. Davey noted that no taxes have been paid to Canada, nor any money reinvested in Canada, by the Buffalo stations.

The senate subsequently approved Bill C-58. Section 3 of the bill which dealt with advertising on television stations, was passed in March, 1976, was granted royal assent on July 16, 1976, and was proclaimed into law on September 22, 1976.[32] There was a grandfather clause in the act that allowed Canadian companies to deduct their U.S. advertising expenditures from their taxable income for a period of up to one year based on contracts that were signed prior to the proclamation of the act. It was not until September 22, 1977, that the bill was fully effective, and all Canadian-placed advertising on U.S. border stations aimed at Canadian audiences were no longer a Canadian tax deductible expense. Advertising placed by Canadian firms on U.S. television stations but aimed primarily at American consumers remained eligible as a deduction against taxable income.

EFFECTS OF BILL C-58

There is a general consensus on both sides of the dispute that Bill C-58 affected the Canadian revenue going to the U.S. border television stations, although the precise amounts vary somewhat depending on the sources.

In the United States

The full brunt of Bill C-58 was not felt until September 1977 because of the grandfathering exception for advertising contracts entered into before implementation in September 1976 and extended for a year. Yet, the short-term effect of Bill C-58 on the Canadian advertising revenues on U.S. border stations was nonetheless termed "drastic" by the border stations in the draft of a memorandum to the U.S. State Department.[33]   From 1975 to 1977, total Canadian advertising revenues, defined as advertising directly primarily to a market in Canada, of the U.S. border stations dropped by 50 percent, the memorandum to the State Department states.

Total Canadian advertising revenues dropped from $18,885,000 in 1975, before the passage or implementation of Section 3 of Bill C-58, to $16,175,000 in 1976 and to $9,175,000 in 1977, according to a survey conducted by Price Waterhouse & Co. among ten affected border broadcasters who represent the bulk of cross-border Canadian advertising revenues. These figures represent total amounts including agency commissions, sales representative commissions and other amounts remaining in Canada. The net amounts paid to U.S. broadcasters, excluding amounts remaining in Canada, also dropped by more than 50 percent, from $14,052,000 in 1975 to $6,133,000 in 1977.[34]

The border stations, in their appeal to the State Department asserted that Bill C-58 "promises to be a more destructive measure" than the earlier cable commercial deletion policy. The cable policy did not gain widespread implementation and it did not attempt to eliminate over-the-air Canadian advertisers from U.S. stations, while Bill C-58 effectively eliminates the competitive effectiveness of a U.S. station as an over-the-air Canadian advertising medium, the border stations contended.[35]

Philip A. Jones, general manager of WGR, Channel 2, commented in personal communication that not only has the extremely higher cost of advertising on border stations reduced Canadian air time, but he added two additional considerations: the buyers' natural reluctance for fear that their clients will come under scrutiny of the government in all taxable areas, and the buyers' concern about indulging in areas where they don't have complete control or complete understanding, Bill C-58 having definitely created a vagueness in their minds.[36]

Despite the losses to the Buffalo stations, indications were that overall profitability by the corporate owners of the Buffalo broadcast units remained healthy. Jones noted:

To offset the loss of Canadian revenues, we have put a more assertive effort toward the local advertisers in the Buffalo market. We have also increased our national spot business to help the decrease in Canadian revenues. The positive effects for the United States advertisers have been very good because of our decrease in Canadian revenues and our bottom line position should not be affected.[37]

In the border stations' memorandum to the State Department, a statement in a letter of November 8, 1977, to U.S. Senator Schweiker (and apparently to other U.S. senators), from Canadian ambassador Peter Towe, was discounted. Towe asserted the financial impact of Bill C-58 on the three network-affiliated stations had been "minimal." The border stations' memorandum asserted:

His [Towe's] evidence for this assertion consisted of excerpts from the corporate annual reports to two Buffalo licenses and a trade magazine's interview with an official of a third Buffalo station. These materials reveal, at most, that (1) the Buffalo stations have succeeded to some degree in making good of the loss of Canadian revenues by selling more time to local Buffalo advertisers; and (2) the loss of Canadian revenues, however substantial, does not threaten the overall viability of Buffalo licensees such as Capital Cities Communication (owners of WKBW-TV, Channel 7), which operate many other television and radio stations, as well as non-broadcast enterprises.[38]

In Canada

The Canadian Department of Communication commissioned a consultant, Donner and Lazar Research Associates of Toronto, to determine how effective Bill C-58 had been. In a press release issued by the department,[39] communications minister David MacDonald announced on September 26, 1979, that the study carried out for the department had found that the controversial tax amendment had achieved a principal objective of redirecting Canadian advertising revenue to Canadian broadcasters and has been "particularly beneficial to newly licensed television stations." The tax measure, the press release states, had reduced the annual flow of funds to the U.S. border stations from $21.5 million in 1975 to $6.5 million in 1978. The Donner and Lazar study, the press release noted, "emphasized the importance of the government's measure to the financial viability of the Canadian commercial television broadcasting sector." The main beneficiaries cited were CITY-TV in Toronto, CKGC, the Global Television Network, CKVU-TV in Vancouver; CITY-TV in

Edmonton, and CKND-TV in Winnipeg. (All but one of these are in the principal areas of coverage of U.S. border stations.)

The Donner and Lazar study, The Impact of the 1976 Income Tax Amendment on United States and Canadian TV Broadcasters, concurred with the border stations that the act had "a rather dramatic financial impact" on the border broadcasters.[40] The study found a 51 percent drop in gross revenue between 1975 and 1977.   Gross Canadian advertising revenue was estimated to have declined from $21.5 million in 1975 to $10.5 million in 1977.[41]

Buffalo's Canadian revenues were estimated by Donner and Lazar to have declined from $9.5 million in 1975 to $5.1 million in 1977, KVOS from $6.7 million in 1975 to $3.4 million in 1977, and the other border stations markets from $5.3 million in 1975 to about $2 million in 1977.[42]

Donner and Lazar stated, "it would appear reasonable" that private Canadian stations, in total, received a net repatriation of Canadian-placed advertising from U.S. border of somewhere in the range of $9 to $10 million in 1977.[43] A significant proportion flowed directly, however, into operating income rather than to increase Canadian production or to improve the quality of the Canadian programming. The consultants stated:

> It did not appear that the repatriated advertising revenues resulted in a major increase in budget allocations for Canadian programming.[44]

Rather, it was reasoned, the repatriated revenue significantly helped the five fledgling stations to survive and grow. Donner and Lazar stated the "main beneficiaries" of the repatriated funds were these stations, whose air time sales increased 40 percent over the period 1975-77. In turn, the consultants state these stations increased their purchase of American shows and at higher prices due to the increased Canadian competition.[45] The report noted there was a "rather large outflow" of the additional revenue accrued by the Canadian broadcasters to Hollywood producers for movies between 1975-77. For example, of the $25.2 million of additional air time sales received by the five stations from 1975-77, 16.3 percent went into domestic programming while 20 percent went towards the purchase of feature films and syndicated programs, the majority of which was purchased in the United States.[46] The consultants added:

> Thus, it is conceivable that while Bill C-58 did generate a substantial repatriation of advertising revenues from United States border stations to Canadian broadcasters, at the same time, because of the intensified competition, a substantial proportion of these additional revenues flowed back to the United States to purchase American programs.[47]

The argument is made, however, that since the new stations are required by the CRTC to have 60 percent Canadian content, the cultural objective would be met. Donner and Lazar state:

> The creation of five new television stations in Canada, together with the 60 percent Canadian content rule guarantees an increased volume of Canadian programming. Even if ratings are dismal at first, the increased fragmentation brought about by these new stations will also insure an increase, albeit a marginal one, in the viewing of Canadian programs by Canadian viewers.[48]

Bill C-58 did appear to increase advertising rates, but not to the extent to which they were out of line with the increases in network time in the United States, and there was not a general squeezing out of local advertisers, although it did occur in the Toronto market.[49] Suggestions by the Buffalo stations for a production fund or taxes in lieu of Bill C-58 were rejected by Donner and Lazar as not providing as much in revenue as Bill C-58.[50]

RECAP

The last two sections have sought to narrate the Canadian advertising controls put in place in the period 1971 to 1976--commercial deletion and income tax legislation Bill C-58. The U.S. border television stations--principally the three in Buffalo and one in Bellingham--led battles to turn the two advertising controls back. Strategies included litigation in the Canadian courts, threats to jam signals to Canada, lobbying by paid counsel in both Ottawa and Washington, and diplomatic and political talks between high levels of both governments. None of the strategies resolved issues, however. Although new instances of commercial deletion were suspended, it was only done when Canada was virtually assured of Bill C-58 passage. As an expression of economic nationalism, Bill C-58 was effective in repatriating millions of dollars to Canadian broadcasters. It was not as effective in the context of its cultural objective, however. The repatriated funds were not used to increase Canadian programming per se but, in fact, there was an increase in the purchase of Hollywood and New York produced programming. Five fledgling Canadian stations were assisted in surviving and growing, and, since they have a requirement of 60 percent Canadian content, it is argued the Canadian cultural mission is assisted, since the U.S. border stations do not have this requirement. Since implementation of Bill C-58, the border stations have mounted a campaign to have it repealed; this second phase, from 1976 to the present, will be presented in the next four sections.

NOTES

1. Harry J. Boyle, letter to Canadian senator Keith Davey, read into record of the Debates of the Senate, 1st session, 30th Parliament, vol. 123, no. 207, June 29, 1976, p. 2298.

2. Time and Reader's Digest in Canada together overwhelmed the Canadian magazine market by being exempt from a previous tax law (in 1965) making advertising in foreign magazines nondeductible. Time and Reader's Digest in Canada received nearly half of the $39 million in advertising revenue of all the major Canadian consumer magazines in 1974. The Canadian edition of Time in 1975 had a circulation of 550,000, or twice the readership of all its native Canadian competitors combined. Reader's Digest at the same time had a circulation of 1.5 million in Canada. Time exemption was eliminated, through Bill C-58, and Time subsequently abandoned its Canadian edition. But, at the same time, Time reduced its advertising rates to compensate and made more money, despite its lower circulation, than it did with the Canadian edition through printing its standard edition with Canadian ads and mailing them at Canada's subsidized second-class postal rates. Reader's Digest, on the other hand, although still substantially American controlled, was granted Canadian status by creating a Canadian branch plant owned by Canadians [see Stephen Clarkson, Canada and the Reagan Challenge: Crisis in Canadian-American Relationship (Toronto: James Lorimer & Co., 1982)].

3. CAB Statement "Bill C-58 and the Proposed Change to Strengthen the Canadian Broadcasting System," to the Canadian House of Commons Standing Committee on Broadcasting, Films and Assistance to the Arts. December 2, 1975, p. 2.

4. Ibid.

5. Ibid.

6. Ibid.

7. Ibid.

8. Ibid., p. 3.

9. Harry J. Boyle, chairman of CRTC. An address entitled "Survival" to the Men's Canadian Club of London, Ontario, December 3.

10. Minutes of Proceedings and Evidence of the Canadian Standing Committee on Broadcasting, Films and Assistance to the Arts, Canadian House of Commons, no. 29, December 1, 1975.

11. Debates of the Canadian senate, 1st session, 30th Parliament, vol. 123, no. 179, April 6, 1976, p. 2299.

12. Minutes of the House of Commons, p. 10.

13. Ibid., p. 11.

14. Ibid., pp. 10-11.

15. The ten largest advertisers in Canada in 1976 were: Proctor and Gamble, General Foods, the government of Canada, General Motors, Colgate-Palmolive, Warner-Lambert, Bristol-Myers, Kraft, Molson, and Ford. See debates of the Canadian senate, 1st session, 30th Parliament, vol. 123, no. 162, March 3, 1976, p. 97.

16. Minutes of House of Commons, pp. 10-11.

17. Ibid., pp. 27-29.

18. Ibid.

19. Ibid., p. 29-30.

20. Ibid., p. 12.

21. Ibid., p. 29.

22. Ibid., pp. 7, 9, 12, 13, 19.

23. Debates of the Canadian senate, 1st session, 30th Parliament, vol. 123, no. 162, March 3, 1976, p. 1843.

24. Ibid., p. 1842.

25. Ibid.

26. Debates of the Canadian senate, 1st session, 30th Parliament, vol. 123, no. 165, March 3, 1976, p. 1872.

27. Debates of the Canadian senate, 1st session, 30th Parliament, vol. 123, no. 179, April 6, 1976, pp. 2026-2027.

28. Debates of the Canadian senate, 1st session, 30th Parliament, vol. 123, no. 162, March 3, 1976, p. 2298.

29. Ibid.

30. Ibid.

31. Minutes of House of Commons, pp. 22-29.

32. Section 3 of Bill C-58 (1st session, 13th Parliament, 23-24 Elizabeth II, 1974-75) became Section 19.1(1) of the Income Tax Act, July 16, 1976. Jeanne Sauve, then Canadian minister of communications, stated the bill would be put into effect when it had been determined that sufficient advertising time was available on Canadian television stations to satisfy Canadian needs. Input from Canadian advertisers and broadcasters were received to August 16, 1976, and the bill was implemented on September 22, 1976.

33. Memorandum to the U.S. States Department. Draft prepared by border stations' counsel and distributed to the border stations, 1978, p. 4. Final copy filed March 30.

34. Ibid., p. 5. See also Complaint filed under Section 301 of the Tract Act of 1974, August 29, 1978, p. 8.

35. Ibid., p. 6.

36. Philip A. Jones, general manager of Buffalo's WGR Channel 2. Letter to Professor Cassata, State University of New York at Buffalo, May 9, 1977, p. 1.

37. Ibid., p. 2.

38. Memorandum, p. 7.

39. Canadian Department of Communication Press Release, September 29, 1979, p. 1.

40. Arthur Donner and Fred Lazar, The Impact of the 1976 Income Tax Amendment on United States and Canadian TV Broadcasters, January, 1979, p. I-3; IV.

41. The border broadcasters hired a consultant to review the Donner and Lazar study. Franklin M. Fisher of the Massachusetts Institute of Technology cast doubts on the analysis because of the methodological problems, including the lack of casting the analysis from a statistical model.

42. Donner and Lazar, p. ii.

43. Ibid., p. III-14.

44. Ibid., p. III-33.

45. Ibid., p. III-14.

46. Ibid., p. III-19.

47. Ibid.
48. Ibid., p. III-18.
49. Ibid., p. III-21.
50. Ibid., p. III-34, 35.

Part III
Border Stations Respond

4
Initial Moves

The U.S. border stations continued, to 1988, to seek the repeal or modification of Bill C-58 after its passage in the fall of 1976. The next four sections relate the events from early 1977 to mid-1988. Although Bill C-58 was proclaimed into law in September 1976, it wasn't fully implemented until one year later, in September 1977. The time lag was to allow advertisers to procure air time on Canadian stations and work out schedules, since, unlike the United States, air time availabilities in Canada are scarce and often booked a year in advance. The lead time also gave the border broadcasters time to feel the revenue pinch and plan a strategy to change Canada's mind on Bill C-58.

THE STRATEGY

The border stations' strategy was two-fold: negotiation and retaliation, the latter often linked to thwarting a Canadian interest related to the broadcast dispute but usually in some area of commerce. In the very early stages, negotiation was the principal modus operandi, but it quickly shifted to secondary status as the border broadcasters found little inclination by the Canadian government to negotiate Bill C-58. Retaliation was deployed to soften Canada up to a point that the border stations thought Canada might negotiate; if such turned out not to be the case, retaliation was reinstituted.

The strategy of retaliation, however, had both proponents and opponents among the border broadcasters. One camp sought negotiations; the other retaliation. The result was some change in the leadership of the battle and on increasing the number of actors involved; that is, the number of stations actively involved in the dispute. Two of the Buffalo stations, WKBW, Channel 7, then owned by Taft Broadcasting Co., and WGR, Channel 2, then owned by Capital Cities Communication held to the negotiating position. WBEN, which was sold in the fall of 1977 to Howard Publications and changed its call letter to WIVB,[1] continued as a leader of the retaliationists, as did Wotmeco, owners of KVOS in Bellingham. Wotmeco and WIVB and a dozen other border stations led assaults on Bill C-58 during this phase of the dispute. WKBW, WGR, and six other border stations kept to the negotiation path. Regardless of the route, the goals of the border stations directly involved--up to twenty-four in this phase of the dispute--remained steadfast. By 1980, the border stations reported they had lost $100 million in Canadian revenue because of Bill C-58.

KISSINGER'S LETTER

One of the first concerted political efforts at implementing the negotiation-retaliation "double-punch" strategy was put into effect in the U.S. Senate.   In July 1976, eighteen senators wrote to U.S. secretary of state Henry A. Kissinger to move on negotiations and offered a proposed Senate measure to retaliate legislatively if Canada did not seek to bend on Bill C-58.[2]   In part, the letter asked that Kissinger:

> Contact the Canadian government and indicate the United States' interests in proceeding with immediate negotiations on the entire range of Canadian policies adversely affecting the U.S. border stations before Bill C-58 is promulgated.[3]

They added:

> If Canada insists on promulgating Bill C-58, we believe it is appropriate that the United States seriously consider a legislative response.[4]

The senators attached a possible legislative response: The Protection of the United States Broadcasters Against Foreign Interference Act of 1976.[5]   The bill would have amended the U.S. Communications Act of 1934 to include a process by which the FCC could find discrimination, by a foreign government, of U.S. broadcast stations whose signals crossed international boundaries.   The FCC could then ask the President for remedial action: to prohibit importation from the offending nation of feature films, video tape recordings, and records, or to impose an excise tax on these products. The funds from the latter would go to U.S. public broadcasting.[6] Although little came of the proposal at this point in terms of actual legislation, the remedies concerning imports of media products were to resurface subsequently in the border stations' claim that Canada was violating the Trade Act of 1974.

The U.S. State Department efforts were ineffective. The Canadian government in October 1976 informed the State Department that Bill C-58 was a matter of internal Canadian tax policy and was non-negotiable. That was to be Canada's position throughout the dispute.

LINKAGE TO TOURISM

The border stations' first major concrete opportunity to implement retaliation arose in 1977. On January 1, a new U.S. tax law, the Tax Reform Act of 1976. went into effect, and its impact on Canadian tourism was rapid and extremely adverse. The law limited U.S. business tax deductions to no more than two conventions and other meetings in Canada and several other countries, and tightened reporting procedures and allowances.[7] A month after the law went into effect, Jean Chretien in Ottawa, the Canadian industry, trade and commerce minister, announced that the government of Canada had approached the State Department to express concern over the new legislation and asked that Canada be exempted.[8]

The impact of the new law was especially severe since Canada had long been the number one foreign destination for U.S. conventions, conferences, and seminars staged outside the United States, with an estimated earnings in excess of $100 million per year. In 1975, for example, a total of 590,000 U.S. delegates attended meetings in Canada.[9]

Senator Barry Goldwater proposed that the Senate exempt Canada, Mexico, Bermuda, and the Caribbean Islands under legislation then before Congress, the Tax Reduction and Simplification Act of 1977. The border stations opposed the exemption unless Canada modified Bill C-58. The border stations' position was complicated, however, for three reasons. First, there was no unanimity among the border stations nor the senators on strategy. Second, the Treasury Department was negotiating with Canada on a new tax treaty in which the convention-tourism issue was being discussed; in fact, in March 1977, before the Senate was to act on the proposed exemption, Canadian finance minister Donald MacDonald expressed optimism that an arrangement, presumably through tax treaty negotiations, might be made to exempt Canada, according to a Canadian Press dispatch.[10] MacDonald's statement followed a meeting with U.S. treasury secretary Michael Blumenthal. Third, the Carter administration was also drafting an easing of the convention limit issue.

Canada, meanwhile, was told that if it was to expect relief through Congress, it should be aware of concerns about Bill C-58. On March 29, 1977, Juanita Krepps, then U.S. secretary of commerce, met with her Canadian counterpart and staffs from both departments for talks that included Canada's desire to have the convention section of the new law modified.[11]   The relative Canadian section had gone into effect just three months before this meeting, and already Canada had estimated it lost at least $12 million in convention cancellations. In the government-to-government talks, Krepps told Canadian industry, trade and commerce minister Chretien that an analogy could be made to the border broadcast issue. She noted that congressional leaders, who would have to modify the U.S. Internal Revenue Code through the Tax Reduction and Simplification Act of 1977 were aware of the broadcasters' difficulties arising from Bill C-58.[12]

A few weeks after this meeting, the border stations drafted their position: it would be inconsistent and inequitable for Canada to demand nondiscrimination with respect to the application of U.S. tax laws relating to foreign conventions, while Canada continued to "discriminate blatantly" against what were seen as the legitimate commercial interests of the U.S. broadcasters.[13] If Canada was to be exempt, it should be on the condition of repeal in Section 3, the border stations contended in a position paper.[14]   One route was through an amendment that the deduction would not be allowed in a country that discriminates against U.S. broadcast stations. Another would exempt Canada only temporarily. Canada would receive a six-month exemption, at the end of which Congress would review the progress Canada had made on modifying the impact of Bill C-58 on U.S. broadcasters.   Congress could then permanently remove the limitations on the deductibility of expenses for conventions.[15] This tactic would meet the needs of U.S. broadcasters by "providing crucial leverage," according to Bart Fisher, Washington counsel for the border stations.[16]

TWO-PRONGED MANEUVER

On April 27, 1977, the Senate debated and voted on whether to grant an exemption to Canada and the other three nations. The result was an apparent two-pronged Congressional maneuver of conciliation toward Canada, with hopes that Canada would respond in kind. The border stations' proposed amendments were not introduced on the Senate floor; however, the six-month exemption tactic would surface more than a year later in a House Committee recommendation.

Although the broadcasters wanted the Senate to tie a Canadian exemption to the broadcast issue, Senator Barry Goldwater felt the two issues were not analogous, but he expressed empathy for the broadcaster's views. He pointed out that Canadian tourism brings in a half billion dollars annually more than Americans spend in Canada, and he did not plan to alter his amendment. Rather, his position was one that relief was needed for Mexico.[17]

Four senators from states that included border stations criticized Canada for Bill C-58; yet when the vote was taken, three supported relief for Canada and one opposed it. Relief (repeal of Section 274(h) of the Internal Revenue Code) was rejected, however, 48-43. Senator Patrick Moynihan and Senator Jacob Javits, both of New York, and Senator Warren Magnuson of Washington, supported relief to Canada, while Senator Dick Schweiker of Pennsylvania voted against it.[18] Moynihan, however, during the debate on the exemption for Canada noted that the next day he and more than twenty other senators were to ask the Senate to pass a measure that would call President Carter's attention to the fact that the Canadian government had adopted a measure in its Internal Revenue Code adversely affecting the flow of commerce between Canadian businesses and American broadcasters (Bill C-58).[19] "We hope," Moynihan stated, "the President will address himself to this serious question with a view to adjusting these outstanding differences through the diplomatic process."[20] Moynihan added that the adoption of the Canadian convention exemption would be "an important gesture," and stated that the convention exemption "prejudices our relations--indeed it can be thought to have the quality of an unfriendly act towards neighbors with whom we have especially close and cherished relation."[21]

Schweiker, noting that a television station in Erie, Pa. suffered an 80 percent decrease in its ad revenue from Canada due to Bill C-58, stated: "The measure grew out of the wave of nationalism which swept over Canada some time ago . . . . [and] until the Canadian government demonstrates a willingness to enter into serious discussions on the question of C-58, no serious consideration should be given by the government to facilitate convention travel by Americans in Canada."[22]

On April 29, 1977, Moynihan introduced the Senate call for Carter to discuss the border broadcast issue with Canada to seek a resolution, and the Senate agreed.[23] In the discussion, Javits asserted that Canada had treated the United States "very roughly" in this matter. "We should make it crystal clear that we do not appreciate the idea that the United States broadcasters should be so blatantly discriminated against by the tax laws of Canada." Moynihan noted that the issue was not just one of commercial interest, but also "the much larger and more important matter of free communication between our two countries."[24]

In Moynihan's statement appears the first formal instance of raising a commercial issue to a broader realm--to the free flow of information across borders. The senator stated:

If there is one thing which has contributed to the fact that this is indeed--and never we forget it--the longest undefended border in the world, it is that people and ideas have moved back and forth across the border freely and openly for a century and a half and more. One may say that, simply by cutting out advertising, we have only stopped one aspect of information. But we know enough about our world to know that, when you begin stopping any kind of information, you have commenced a process that never should have begun, and one about which one can never make a decision as to where it will end.[25]

Magnuson, in addressing the senators, documented that the strategy at this stage was negotiation; he indicated retaliation was considered but that the conciliatory option was selected:

Consideration had been given to acting in retaliation by tying the issue of Canadian tax discrimination against U.S. broadcasters to the amendment to the tax bill which would have allowed Americans to deduct as business expenses conventions that might be held in Canada. But we thought a better way to get at the latter was to express the sense of the Senate in no uncertain terms about this major irritation that has been going between us and Canada for some time.[26]

Although the Moynihan amendment originally linked Bill C-58 and the foreign convention tax provisions, the amendment that was passed solely requested the president to raise with the Canadians the problems created by Bill C-58. It was referred to the Committee on Foreign Relations. In May 1977, the proposed resolution was sent to the U.S. State Department for comment. A reply was received in July. The department didn't object to the resolution, and the Senate Foreign Relations Committee felt "it would be useful" for the State Department to have the committee's indication of support. The State Department had written to the committee that it considered it "unlikely that it [Canada] will alter the tax policy in question. Nevertheless, it is our intention to keep this matter and its adverse impact on United States broadcast interest before the Canadian government as opportunities to do so arise."[27] In August 1977, the committee discussed the resolution and by voice vote, and without dissent, ordered it to be reported favorably. The Senate adopted the resolution on September 8, 1977. However, the resolution ran into a problem in the House because it was expressed as the "sense of the Senate" that Carter should act.

Repeal of the tax deduction limit for Canada did not die. Efforts were being made not only in the Senate but also in the House to get the exemption approved. Border stations' counsel, meanwhile, were actively seeking to prevent the exemption. The border stations had apparently coalesced on the retaliation strategy because the previous congressional maneuver had not brought corresponding conciliation on Bill C-58 in Ottawa.

Edward J. Hummers, counsel for the border broadcasters in Washington, reported that he and a representative of an Oregon station spent June 28 on Capitol Hill.[28] They were "seeking information concerning and lobbying against" the repeal of the provision limiting the deductibility of convention expenses, on behalf of WBEN.[29] They met with Representative Al Ullman to pursue a rumor that the Canadians had convinced him to support the repeal, but Ullman stated that he had not been contacted by the Canadians and expressed very little personal interest in the repeal measure, according to Hummers. They also met with an aide to Senator Packwood and spent a substantial amount of time with the assistant chief of staff of a joint Senate-House committee dealing with taxation matters.[30]

Hummers confirmed a coalescing of efforts to block the repeal of the Canadian convention exemption. He reported that counsel for all the border stations had met on June 30 and were now unanimous in a strategy of seeking to block the Canadian tax exemption.[31] Hummers stated, "Surprisingly, all agreed to pursue the defeat of any repeal of the existing provision." He confirmed that the dominant strategy had turned to retaliation.

Canadian sources continue to inform us that amendment or repeal of C-58 in the near future is not likely. Our best bet is to continue to present the Canadians with as many difficulties in Washington as is possible with the hope that C-58 becomes so vexing to the Government that an alternative to their 'cultural dominance' syndrome will be found.[32]

FLUID SITUATION

The problem with holding to the rejection of the Canadian deduction was that it wasn't solely in the hands of Congress and subject to direct lobbying efforts. There were other actors in the dispute. There was movement on the other two fronts: The administration was heading towards easing the restrictions regarding conventions in Canada, and talks were continuing towards easing the regulation in the drafting of the new tax treaty between the two countries.

On the first, Hummers reported:

The most distressing news involves the Administration's possible tax reform package now being written by the Treasury. Option papers are expected to got to the President in mid-August with the President sending a message to Congress later in September [1977]. The hotel industry is pushing for modification of the present convention limitations which would reduce the amount of paper work and permit one foreign convention a year. If the Administration's proposal reaches a reasonable compromise, it is likely that amendment would pass the Senate and House and we will lose a weapon against the Canadians.[33]

On the second, support for the tax treaty route mounted and the convention issue was discussed in June 1977 at a Canadian-U.S. interparliamentary conference held in Victoria, British Columbia. "The final consensus of the group was that each side urge its representatives to the United States-Canada Tax Treaty negotiations to approach both of these matters [C-58 and the convention issue] from the possible standpoint of the adoption of broad non-discrimination language in a tax treaty," according to a participant, U.S. representative Lloyd Meeds.[34]

The non-discrimination language would mean that taxes would apply equally to nationals and non-residents; to the border stations, non-discrimination meant the repeal or modification of Bill C-58. It appeared, following the conference, that the U.S. State Department was going to seek to link the two issues in the treaty talks. Richard D. Vine, a State Department deputy assistant secretary for Canadian affairs, stated that the department "welcomed" the sense of the resolution the interparliamentary group arrived at, adding: "We understand that the U.S. and Canadian negotiators working on the revision of the bilateral tax treaty are investigating the possibility of dealing with the C-58 and convention expenses problem within the tax treaty context."[35]

With the multifaceted moved underway as 1977 drew towards a close, Canada continued to feel the effects of the lack of an exemption on tourism. There were 109 U.S. conventions cancelled by August 1977, for a loss of $35 million.[36]

As 1978 began, then vice president Walter Mondale announced in Ottawa that restrictions on foreign conventions in Canada would be eased.[37] On January 17, Mondale made the changes known after a meeting with Prime Minister Trudeau and Canadian Cabinet ministers. The restrictions would eliminate the two convention limit, ease attendance and reporting requirements; the proposal held no relief, however, for the border broadcasters. Again in May 1978, the State Department protested Bill C-58. In August, the Canadian government again stated that Bill C-58 was non-negotiable. Accordingly, the State Department conceded that further attempts to raise the issue of Bill C-58 with Canadian officials would be unproductive and might hamper the resolution of other differences between the two countries.

NOTES

1. The ownership of WBEN in Buffalo changed September 16, 1977. It had been owned by the Buffalo Evening News and was sold in April 1977 to Blue Chip Stamps Company (Warren Buffet). The FCC's rules on cross-channel ownership disallowed a print medium and a broadcast medium in the same market. WBEN was purchased by Howard Publications, and the call letters changed to WIVB. In mid-1988, the station was sold again.

2. U.S. senators signing the letter were: Warren G. Magnuson, Henry M. Jackson, John Tower, Bill Brock, Harrison Williams, Dick Schweiker, Patrick Leahy, Richard Stone, Howard Baker, Lawton Vhiles, Jesse Helms, Robert Stafford, James B. Allen, John Tunney, Hugh Scott, Jacob Javits, James L. Buckley, and Hubert H. Humphrey.

3. Henry A. Kissinger. Letter to the U.S. secretary of state from eighteen U.S. senators, July 27, 1976, p. 1

4. Ibid., p. 2.

5. U.S. Senate draft bill, 94th Congress, 2nd Session, not numbered, July 21, 1976.

6. Ibid., pp. 1-3.

7. What Canada and several other countries viewed as inequities derived from the Tax Reform Act of 1976. Section 602 added Section 274(h) to the Internal Revenue Code of 1954. It: (1) permits an individual U.S. taxpayer to take tax deductions for expenses in attending up to two foreign conventions annually, provided the taxpayer attends at least two-thirds of the scheduled sessions; (2) limits deductions for subsistence expenses at foreign conventions to the per diem allowances used by U.S. government officials; (3) limits travel deductions to an amount equal to regular coach fare and provides that even this amount can be fully deducted only if at least half of the days are devoted to business-related activities; and (4) requires an attendance record of all sessions attended by the individual delegate to be provided, authorized, and kept by the association concerned. Senators Barry Goldwater, Inouye and Dennis DeConcini proposed to repeal Section 274(h) and introduced Amendment 195 to the Internal Revenue Code, which would insert Section 408, "Restoring the Deductibility of Expenses for Attending Certain Conventions in the North America Area." In addition to Canada, Mexico, Bermuda, and the Caribbean Islands would be exempted. The Goldwater exemption was introduced as Congress was considering H.R. 3477, the Tax Reduction and Simplification Act, which called for changes in the 1976 Tax Reform Act (see Congressional Record, Proceedings and Debates of the 95th Congress, 1st Session, vol. 123, no. 7, April 27, 1977.)

8. Canadian Office of Tourism, press release, February, 1977, p. 2.

9. Ibid.

10. Canadian Press (CP), "Reciprocal deal possible on tax laws," The Chronicle (Halifax, N.S.) Herald, March 9, 1977.

11. Congressional Record, reprint of April 15, 1977, letter from Juanita Krepps, U.S. secretary of commerce, to Senator Warren G. Magnuson, vol. 23, no. 70, April 27, 1977, p. S6765.

12. Ibid.

13. Position paper prepared by border stations, April 15, 1977, p. 3.

14. Ibid.

15.   Proposed Foreign Conventions Amendment, 1977, prepared by Bart Fisher, border stations' counsel, for senators Goldwater and Inouye, April 13, 1977, p. 2.

16.   Ibid., p. 3.

17.   Congressional Record, Proceedings and Debates of the 95th Congress, 1st Session, vol. 123, no. 7, April 27, 1977, p. S6568.

18.   Ibid., p. S6569.

19.   Representative Henry J. Nowak, who represents the Buffalo area, stated in a letter on May 26 that, at the request of Leslie Arries, Jr., Nowak contacted Senator Moynihan in April to relay the broadcasters' concern about the Goldwater amendment and the ensuing amendment offered by Moynihan. Following the two Senate moves in April, Nowak added his perspective: "While Congressional action is still an option, it would have graver and wide consequences than merely legislative retaliation for an unfair Canadian policy towards our border stations, and it is to be hoped that diplomatic efforts will result in a permanent, mutually satisfactory solution for the problem" (see Henry J. Nowak letter to Mary B. Cassata, State University of New York at Buffalo, May 26, 1977).

20.   Congressional Record, op. cit., p. S6566.

21.   Ibid.

22.   Ibid., p. S6568-69.

23.   Amendment 228 was proposed by senators Moynihan, Young, Stafford, Magnuson, Metcalf, Javits, Schweiker, Williams, Helms, Anderson, Gravel, Schmitt, Burdick, Melcher, Chiles, Sasses, Allen, Riegle, Jackson, Griffin, Leahy, Bentsen, Stone, Heinz, Goldwater and Roth. The amendment was subsequently drafted as a resolution, S. Res. 152, and was referred to the Committee on Foreign Relations (see Proceedings and Debates of the 95th Congress, 1st Session, vol. 123, no. 7, April 29, 1977, pp. S6762-63).

24.   Ibid., p. S6763.

25.   Ibid.

26.   Ibid., p. S6764.

27.   U.S. Senate Committee on Foreign Relations, letter from the U.S. State Department, July, 1977, p. 3.

28.   Edward J. Hummers, Jr., was with the law firm of Fletcher, Heald, Kenehan & Hildreth of Washington, D.C. Other counsel for the border stations during this phase of the dispute (1976-83) included in Washington: Cordon & Jacob; Patton, Boggs, & Blow; Cohn & Marks; Preson, Thorgrimson, Eillis, Holman & Fletcher; Smith & Pepper; former Senator Charles Goodell; Mullin, connor & Rhyne; Fisher, Wayland, Southmayd & Cooper; Stambler & Strinsky; Fowler & Meyers. Counsel in Ottawa included: Intercounsel; Hewitt, Hewitt & Nesbitt & Reid; Gowling & Henderson. A public relations firm was also hired in 1978: Hill & Knowlton, Inc. of Washington.

29.   Edward J. Hummers, Jr., letter to Leslie G. Arries, Jr., July 7, 1977, p. 1.

30.   Mark L. McConaghy, assistant chief of staff of the Joint Committee on Taxation, one of the few joint Senate-House committees. Edward J. Hummers, Jr., noted that the joint committee permits greater interplay between the House and Senate and uses a separate staff, expert in tax issues and familiar with the personal interests of the involved senators and representatives (see Hummers, p. 2).

31.   Hummers, p. 2.

32. Ibid.

33. Ibid., p. 3.

34. Lloyd Meeds, a U.S. representative to the Canadian-U.S. interparliamentary conference, June 1977. Letter to Lawrence N. Woodworth, assistant to the treasury for tax policy, June 16, 1977, p. 1.

35. Richard D. Vine, deputy assistant secretary for Canadian Affairs of the State Department, letter to Senator Meeds, July 8, 1977, p. 2.

36. John King, "Restrictions on Foreign Conventions Eased, U.S. Move Worth Millions to Canada," The Globe and Mail, January 28, 1978, p. 12.

37. Ibid.

5
New Tacks

By the summer of 1978, the border stations' situation seemed unchanged. Initiatives had been made, political action was taken--but Canada remained adamant. Washington attorney Alfred C. Cordon, one of the stations' chief operatives during this phase of the dispute, summarized the state of affairs: "The situation, however, seems to rest today where it was at the time C-58 became effective."[1]

The time seemed right for three additional tacks: Seeking to reject a Canadian exemption to the convention limit before the powerful House Ways and Means Committee; pressing for relief through the tax treaty between the two countries that the Treasury Department was negotiating; and moving ahead on a previously held-in abeyance proposal to charge Canada with a violation of a trade agreement between the two countries (under the Trade Act of 1974).

"WORK" COMMITTEE

The border stations sought, in the summer and fall of 1978, to press in Congress to continue to link the two bilateral issues--border broadcasting and the foreign conventions exemption. Action moved to the House's powerful Ways and Means Committee. The border stations' counsel, the record shows, were very active in working the committee. Letters from counsel indicated appraisals on who had contacted which committee members and where each committee member stood, and provided draft amendments, questions to be asked, and so on. Representatives Barber Conable and Lloyd Meeds, committee members favoring the linkage tactic, both urged relief to Canada should be on the condition of relief from Bill C-58.

There were indications, however, that the two Buffalo television stations were not as active at this stage as other border stations would have hoped. Alfred Cordon, a Washington attorney for WIVB (formerly WBEN), stated:

> I believe both Taft [owners of WKBW] and Capital Cities [owners of WGR] have been maintaining a low profile on this. We were previously informed that Taft planned no activity because they have other Canadian business activity. Capital Cities seems to be indulging in a low profile.[2]

The low profiles involved Taft's plans to build a $105 million theme park near Toronto.[3]

Cordon noted that Conable would offer an amendment which would: "incorporate language developed by us [the border stations' counsel] requiring the President to take action in the event that a foreign country discriminates in a manner affecting the commerce of the United States. ... quite a large-sized victory for our side."[4]

Conable did introduce the amendment to ease the convention limit, but only if a foreign country was found not to be pursuing a policy of trade discrimination aimed at U.S. citizens, including corporate citizens.

Cordon commented: "Congressman Conable, in short, did a masterful job of handling the procedural aspects of his presentation and our proposal conceived earlier was unanimously adopted by the committee in a voice vote."[5]

In October 1978, the Ways and Means Committee added amendments to legislation that would deny the North American exemption to a foreign country whose income tax laws contained provisions analogous to those of Bill C-58, which affect U.S. commerce, upon certification by the President that the foreign government was unwilling to negotiate with respect to an adjustment of its income tax system. The committee stated: "It would be inappropriate to afford special treatment for conventions held outside the United States if the tax laws of the country in question discriminate against U.S. residents."[6]

The bill would give Canada and Mexico full exemptions, but, in Canada's case, only for six months from the time the bill became law. If during that period Ottawa didn't negotiate a better deal for the border broadcasters, Canada would lose the foreign convention exemption.[7] The committee's proposal paralleled the position taken in April 1977 by the border broadcasters in a position paper.

The continued congressional pressure riled Canadian officials.[8] Linking Bill C-58 and the convention reprieve, Jeanne Sauve said, resulted in a "bartering game where we are not discussing each matter on its merits. We have not wanted to discuss it this way." Jack

Horner, Canada's new minister of industry, trade and commerce, referring to Bill C-58, added, "It is our country, and we should be able to regulate what is deductible." Horner contended that his ministry would try to negotiate a settlement but warned that if the U.S. tax amendment squeezes Canadian convention revenues, there was the possibility that Canada would put restrictions on its citizens seeking to visit the United States. "I wouldn't want things to escalate," he asserted.

On pressing for relief through the tax treaty, the border stations were seeking language in the treaty that would provide relief from Bill C-58 by an agreement on no discrimination in taxing between Canadian nationals and non-residents (the border stations). A brief pressing this approach was presented by counsel for Wotmeco, owners of KVOS in Bellingham, at a U.S. Treasury Department hearing in December 1978.

Charging Canada with a violation of the Trade Act of 1974, Wotmeco had shelved the proceeding,[9] but in July 1978 Cordon indicated that the owners of KVOS "may be changing its mind."[10] Cordon indicated, however, that the owners of WKBW in Buffalo, "will not join us, based on earlier statements," and that Capital Cities, owners of WGR in Buffalo, would not.

301 COMPLAINT FILED

A month later, on August 29, 1978, representatives for thirteen U.S. border stations filed a complaint with U.S. Trade representative Robert Strauss.[11] The stations alleged that Section 3 of Bill C-58 was a discriminatory tax policy and an unreasonable barrier to U.S trade.

Speaking on behalf of the border stations at a press conference in Washington, D.C., were Leslie G. Arries, Jr., president of WBEN (which was to become WIVB the following month upon the sale to Howard Publications), and Richard Wolfson, executive vice president of Wotmeco Enterprises, and licensee of KVOS. They said they were requesting that the president impose duties or other import restrictions on the products or services of Canada until "the discriminatory taxing situation is satisfactorily resolved." The U.S. border stations contended that rebuffs by the Canadian government to negotiate had brought them to seek this remedy.[12]

The border stations' action was taken under Section 301 of the Trade Act of 1974 which authorizes the president to retaliate against unfair trade practices of other nations that restrict imports from the United States or that discriminate against or harm U.S. commerce. To be actionable, such practices may be either unreasonable, illegal under international law, or inconsistent with the international obligations of the restricting country. Examples of unfair trade practices under Section 301 are import quotas, variable levies, taxes that discriminate against imports, licensing systems, and discriminary rules. Section 301 extends protection to both U.S. goods and services associated with international trade.[13] The border stations' contention was that broadcasting was a service falling within the 301 definition. The U.S. administrative agency with primary responsibility for a decision was the Section 301 Committee of the Trade Policy Review Group. The latter is part of the Office of the Special Representative for Trade Negotiations. The committee members included the office of the Special Representative for Trade Negotiations and representatives of the Labor Department, Commerce Department, and the Economic Bureau of the State Department.

The filing of the complaint was heralded at a Washington press conference with attendant media coverage, orchestrated by the border stations' newly hired public relations firm, Hill and Knowlton of Washington, and more media coverage followed. The day after the filing, Arries, Wolfson, and Bart Fisher, an attorney for the border stations, were scheduled by the public relations firm for appointments with media representatives in Canada.[14]

Specifically, the complaint contended that Section 3 of Bill C-58 discriminated against United States commerce, was an unreasonable and unjustified policy.

Supporting the discrimination claim, the border stations asserted that since the denial of a deduction for income tax purposes applied only to the advertisements placed by a Canadian entity on a foreign broadcasting station, the U.S. originated advertisements were subject to a higher tax rate than advertisements from Canadian stations, solely because they were imported.[15] The border stations noted that Bill C-58 had resulted in doubling the cost of U.S. broadcast advertising to Canadian purchasers since the income tax deduction would be about 48 percent, and thus the importation into Canada of advertisements via border stations was discriminated against by use of a tax subsidy that had the effect of a substantial tariff barrier.

The border stations contended Section 3 of Bill C-58 was unreasonable for four reasons.[16] The first was that Canada should pay for services it receives, and not doing so was unreasonable. Section 3 of Bill C-58 permits Canada to obtain benefits while impairing the opportunities of U.S. stations to earn fair compensation in the open, competitive marketplace, the border stations contended. Benefits cited were three-fold: viewers in Canada received the U.S. television programming, Canadian advertisers had the opportunity to market their goods via the border stations, and U.S. programming had built a viable and advanced cable television industry in Canada. Bill C-58, the border stations argued in their complaint, was a strong inducement to Canadian advertisers to shift time from U.S. to Canadian stations so that Canadian viewers obtained the programming without paying for part of its costs through the accompanying Canadian advertising.

The second claim for unreasonableness was that by doubling the cost of U.S. broadcast advertising, Bill C-58 was a discriminatory tax subsidy that had the effect of a prohibitive tariff. The third claim was that the cross-border advertising gained by Canada through Bill C-58 was not reinvested in significant amounts in Canadian programming and were inadequate to establish an improved domestic programming industry. The fourth claim was that Bill C-58 was a unilateral policy that ignored the bilateral character of the telecommunications problem involved.

The border stations' contention that Section 3 of Bill C-58 was unjustifiable was based on an alleged violation of several sections of the General Agreement on Tariffs and Trade (GATT).[17]

In addition, the border stations argued that Section 3 burdens and restricts U.S. commerce. The losses of advertising to border stations were presented as evidence.

REMEDIES PROPOSED

The border stations developed their complaint in a seventy-seven page brief in the fall of 1978 in which they proposed remedies to the President.[18] The border stations suggested the most appropriate remedy would be for Canada to repeal Section 3. If Canada did not repeal Bill C-58, then a similar result could be effected in the context of negotiations for the new tax treaty.[19] If Canada were to refuse to repeal Bill C-58 unilaterally or through tax treaty negotiations, the border stations maintained, Canada should negotiate compromises the border stations were proposing. The first possible compromise involved the establishment by the U.S. border stations of a taxable presence in Canada, under which Canadian revenues would be subject to tax by the Canadian government. A variation of this proposal would be the establishment of a Canadian taxable presence in conjunction with an investment fund that would finance measures designed to stimulate the Canadian program production industry. If neither were acceptable, the border stations stated that the President should raise the level of duties on Canada's program production industry (films, videotape recordings, and sound recordings) and retaliate by changes in the auto pact between the two countries (the U.S.-Canadian Automotive Products Agreement of 1965). The stations estimated that retaliation against feature films, television programs, radio and television programs, radio and television jingles, and recordings would approximate the trade coverage in terms of revenues lost by the U.S. border stations since the passage of Bill C-58 in 1976.

The dollar amount of United States's retaliatory moves was pegged at $100 million by Bart Fisher.[20] The figure was derived from the amount of lost cross-border advertising on an annual basis, the diminished asset value of U.S. stations whose Canadian advertising revenues have stopped as a result of Bill C-58, and punitive damages for the unfair dealing by the government of Canada, according to Fisher.

Since reducing the importation of Canadian cultural products (films, recordings, etc.) would not, in itself, add to the coffers of the border stations, the retaliation must be seen as one to push Canada to negotiate the border stations' compromise proposals. The action further documents the double-punch strategy of retaliation (through linkage to other issues) and negotiations.

CANADIANS RESPOND

Seven days after the border stations filed their expanded brief, public hearings were held before the interagency Section 301 committee considering the complaint.[21] Witnesses included border station representatives and advocates for Canadian broadcasting and cable firms.[22] No Canadian government representatives attended the hearing because the government viewed the session as an internal U.S. government affair, saying that it should not have to defend its policies before a foreign tribunal.[23] Ottawa did ask the U.S. State Department to present a note to the committee saying the 1976 tax law changes do not violate U.S. laws and are needed to protect the Canadian broadcast industry.[24] The Canadian government also filed a statement. The government's statement and briefs by Jerry S. Grafstein, counsel for Rogers Cable TV in Toronto, rebutted the U.S. border stations' complaint point by point.[25] The Canadian government's statement and the Grafstein briefs are strikingly similar in facts and analysis, although the language of the government's statement is not the legal style of a brief; thus, it would appear that attorney Grafstein played a key role in the Canadian government's statement.

Alfred C. Cordon, counsel for the border stations, alluded to a connection after first praising the stations' presentation:

> Our presentation of this subject matter has become quite polished, in light of the fact the subject has been under consideration in other forms. I believe that we got into the record a very good direct case.

> The Rogers presentation was one which seemed designed to ingratiate Rogers with the Liberal Party of the Canadian government. The lawyer's [Grafstein's] appearance may have been the Canadian government's way of appearing in an off-hand manner, since he is reportedly highly placed in the Liberal Party.[26]

One contention by Grafstein in particular struck at the underpinnings of the border stations' case. Rogers's counsel argued that broadcast advertising was not included in the jurisdiction of the Trade Act of 1974, and that Bill C-58 did not qualify as a foreign trade practice. Grafstein contended that broadcast advertising would have to be goods or service involved in international trade, and that broadcast advertising was not involved in international trade because "the clear and unambiguous purpose of Bill C-58 is directed solely to Canadian advertisers wishing to sell goods within Canada."[27]

Grafstein added:

Advertisers by tradition utilize the airwaves in order to facilitate the 'commerce' or 'trade in goods' within a given market [the local license]. Thus the advertising in question is not directed toward U.S. commerce but to Canadian commerce. Advertising directed toward U.S. commerce or trade of the U.S. is not at all affected by the purposes of Bill C-58.[28]

The Section 301 committee questioned whether C-58 was a foreign practice under its jurisdiction, according to a Canadian journalist for the Globe and Mail.[29] Subsequent events bear out the committee's concern as to whether broadcast advertising was covered under the Trade Act of 1974 (it was made clear by revising the act to so state the following year).

TOUGH TO SORT OUT

The journalist also noted that, in the cross-fire of oral and written statements, "The disputing parties weaved such a variety of intricate explanations and arguments that some committee members were left shaking their heads, trying to sort it out."[30]

The border stations' claims were denied by the Canadians. The Canadian government's statement first presented the cultural and social rationale for broadcasting in Canada and then countered specific assertions by the border broadcasters. On the contention that Bill C-58 is discriminatory because it subjects ads from border stations to a higher tax rate than ads from Canadian stations, the government maintained the tax differential is on the Canadian firms--the Canadian advertisers--and not on the American border stations. In regard to the unreasonableness of the allegation that Canada's tax measures impair the opportunities to U.S. stations to earn fair compensation in the open, competitive market, the Canadian government responded that the broadcasting industry in North America is regulated, and regional advertising markets are normally protected by restraints imposed by the relevant body (the FCC or the

CRTC). "In this sense, the openness of the 'marketplace' must be considered limited," the Canadian government maintained.[31]

Regarding the assertation that Canada has built a viable and advanced cable television industry on the strength of carrying U.S. programs, the government contended the point was not relevant to the Section 301 complaint that Bill C-58 violates the trade act.

In regard to the allegation that advertising revenues repatriated from Bill C-58 had not been reinvested in significant amounts in Canadian programming, the government contended it was not relevant to the subject of the complaint but added that C-58 had so far (this was prior to the completion of the Donner and Lazar study) "proved to be an effective mechanism for protecting the existing revenue base in a number of Canadian markets."

The Canadian government denied that it had ignored the bilateral nature of the problem by citing intergovernmental meetings on the issue and denied that C-58 was a violation of GATT.

THE "LOCAL LICENSE"

Representatives of the three Canadian broadcast firms at the hearing, including Moses Znaimer, president of CITY-TV in Toronto, subsequently filed a rebuttal brief in which they concurred with the view that Bill C-58 is not in the jurisdiction of the Trade Act Committee since Section 301 does not encompass services having a connection to international trade.[32]   Much of the brief revolved around the concept of the local license--licenses granted to stations to serve specific local areas--and their view that the local license principle had been breached by the border stations.   The brief excerpts an exchange from the hearing at which Thomas Graham, a member of the Section 301 committee and deputy general counsel of the Office of the Special Representative for Trade Negotiations, asked the border stations whether, "picking up the broadcasts of the border stations, couldn't . . . a long time ago have been construed as piracy of signals if there hadn't been some understanding, again, explicitly, or implicit, that there was some degree or type of compensation for it?"[33]

David Mintz, vice president and general manager of KVOS in Bellingham replied, "Nobody asked us. They took our signals and God bless them, we wanted them to. That was an augmentation (sic) of our potential income."[34]

Nevertheless, the Canadian broadcasters' asserted that the border stations willingness to volunteer a signal into Canada gives them "no right to sell advertising in areas for which they are not licensed to serve" and especially in a foreign country over which their licensing authority, the FCC, has no jurisdiction.

The sales they make or made to Canadian advertisers [for Canadian consumption] are of a windfall nature (since the broadcasters have no obligation to serve the needs and interests of Canadians through production of Canadian programming) and, thus, have no protection under broadcasting law.[35]

The American broadcasters are trying to establish a "right to poach" in Canadian broadcasters' licensed areas as compensation for being carried as distant signals on Canadian systems, the Canadian broadcasters asserted.[36] "Bill C-58 is designed to support the principle of local licence and therefore is both reasonable and justifiable," they maintained.

Edward S. Rogers, president of the 200,000-subscriber cable system, Rogers Cable TV, took a similar position in the hearing:

> We think that it is essential that broadcasters of one country don't think that they are of right entitled to a market in another country for which they clearly are not licensed to serve. . . . Border stations talk about fair competition but are not willing to compete on the same basis, i.e., with 50 percent Canadian programming. And, if they did, the citizens of their own U.S. communities would be concerned by the lack of service to them.[37]

WINDFALL NOT JUSTIFIED

Rogers added that merely because Buffalo stations were able to earn a windfall profit in the past doesn't justify a continuation in the future.

Rogers' counsel, Grafstein, stated that the border broadcasters had failed to note that over the years they had gained in excess of $100 million in windfall revenue at the expense of the Canadian stations, which allowed the border stations "to grow out of proportion" in revenue and profitability to the relative size of their own community markets, which they were licensed to serve. Since the border stations are not subject to the programming cost requirements of the CRTC, they could operate "virtually as vehicles to 'dump' U.S. programs into Canada" and to pick up Canadian audiences and Canadian advertising dollars, the cable counsel charged.[38]

Grafstein stated that Bill C-58 is not discriminatory in that it applies to all broadcasting undertakings not licensed by the CRTC. Bill C-58 is not an unreasonable and unjustifiable non-tariff barrier, Grafstein contended, in that it imposes no duties or restrictions on foreign broadcasting operators but only confers certain tax benefits on Canadian taxpayer corporations that advertise on broadcasting operations licensed by the CRTC.[39]

According to Grafstein:

Bill C-58 merely restores in a financial sense, the marketplace for appropriately licensed broadcasting licensees in order to fulfill their cultural and social responsibilities to the community they serve consistent with Canadian law and Canadian regulatory practice.[40]

DIFFERENT ROUTE

Rogers, in his statement at the hearing, noted the absence of two Buffalo stations. WGR (Taft), WKBW (Capital Cities) and six other border stations were not among the signators to the Section 301 complaint. They did support the facts and analysis in the complaint in a separate statement, but not the strategy of retaliation.[41] The eight stations explained:[42]

We wholeheartedly agree that the Canadian trade practice which is the subject of the complaint constitutes an unreasonable discrimination against U.S. commerce and a burden and restriction on that commerce. At present, however, we are not convinced that the retaliation, which is the only remedy specified by Section 301, would achieve any desired result if recommended by the STR [Special Trade Representative] or imposed by the President.[43]

The eight border stations added they were not convinced that retaliation against Canadian imports would "play a useful role" in persuading the Canadian government to depart from its presently "wholly unreasonable" position that the defense of Canada's cultural interest gives it no choice but to disregard legitimate interests of the U.S. border stations.[44] They concluded:

For the present, therefore, we strongly support efforts to institute negotiations of the general kind described in the complaint, coupled with the continuing efforts by the Canadian government that the issue is one of importance in the relations between the two countries and that in the final analysis no such issue can be considered non-negotiable.[45]

The broadcasters who had filed the complaint reiterated and expanded their position at the hearing. The U.S. National Association of Broadcasters (NAB) presented a statement in support of the border broadcasters.[46] NAB expressed continued opposition to Bill C-58; it did not express an opinion, however, on the remedies proposed in the complaint stating that the NAB had not considered the question of remedy at that point.[47]

Leslie G. Arries, Jr., served on the NAB board and pointed out that the signals of the border stations spilled over into Canada because of the omni directional nature of the antenna radiation, and that the signals from the border stations are in accord with an agreement in 1952 between the two countries (the Canadian-USA Television Agreement of 1952).[48] Arries noted that Canada under the accord could block the border stations' signals and cut out American programming, but chose not to.[49] Rather, Arries stated in a strong criticism of the Canadian cable television industry, that the CRTC specifically authorizes the reception of border stations signals when the CRTC licenses a Canadian cable system. Arries, in effect, argues the border stations are thus licensed in Canada.[50]

Arries contended the Canadian cable industry was using the border stations programming "as the bait" to create the most sophisticated cable industry in the world. The uncompensated Canadian use of the U.S. television station signals as the basis of an extensive cable industry, Arries argued, is "unreasonable and lies at the heart" of the Section 301 complaint.[51]

Arries continued:

We recognize and appreciate the fact that Canada desires to develop a cultural identity of its own but this has nothing to do with the legal criteria of the trade complaint. . . . As long as the government of Canada permits Canadian cable television to extensively carry U.S. television stations, it should not complain about nor seek to stop Canadian business from advertising on U.S. stations. It must be remembered that Canada says it wishes to develop its own cultural identity on the one hand, while at the same time on the other hand, permitting substantial American programming to be seen.[52]

REACTIONS TO 301

The Canadian government's reaction to the Section 301 complaint was steadfast support of Bill C-58. Sauve stood firm. Asked what Canada would do if the U.S. trade representative urged President Carter to take action, Sauve replied, "We'll have to take our lumps."[53] She added:

This money [the $20 million] is important to us. It amounted to more than the net after-tax profits of the entire Canadian TV system. But it's more than just a question of money. The revenues being diverted to U.S. stations were vitally important, particularly to new and developing Canadian stations trying to make a meaningful contribution to the binding together of a vast nation.[54]

Appearing on CBC radio, Sauve was asked "about the latest charge made by the Americans." She replied:

Well, I think their representations [the border stations] sufficiently take into account that one of the very important facts is that they are not regulated to broadcast in Canada. There's a spill-over in Canada but they are not regulated to cover that territory so I don't know why they are bothered by the fact that we have in fact looked after a matter which is completely internal. It's a fiscal matter.[55]

The revenue, she noted, was needed to "produce better television programs."

Sauve's position that Bill C-58 is "none of their [the United States's] business" drew the support of an editorial in the Toronto Star. But, the newspaper urged Canada to use the money to improve Canadian television:

At the same time, she [Sauve] ought to show herself equally demanding that the revenues be used for the stated purpose-- to build up Canada's film and broadcast industries. . . . There is no evidence yet to show that private broadcasting in Canada, or the CBC, have committed a sufficient amount of this additional income toward improving their product.[56]

A similar chord was struck by an editorial in the Vancouver Sun:

Promoting a uniquely Canadian culture is not the equivalent to improving profits on commercial Canadian television stations. The CRTC seems to have the two confused. At the very least, Canadian government actions seem certain to stiffen the Americans' resolve to continue their ban on foreign conventions as an allowable expense.[57]

The Vancouver Sun's editorial suggested that the only practical answer to American programming is popular Canadian programming. "Being nasty to American border stations does more harm than good, much as private Canadian broadcasters may applaud," the editorial concluded.

On the other hand, a major U.S. trade magazine, Broadcasting, questioned the border stations' move. Noting that U.S. stations near the Canadian border are "suffering the effects of nationalist sentiment that has been developing within the government of Canada," the editorial asked, however, whether the border stations were "entirely realistic" in seeking retaliation through the Section 301 complaint.[58] The editorial explained:

Americans justifiably regard it [Bill C-58] as anti-American in the extreme, but however it may be viewed on this [the United States] side of the border, it suits the present Canadian scheme of things. If conditions were reversed, the United States Congress would rise in outrage at foreign intrusion in internal affairs.[59]

The editorial drew a stinging rebuke from the border stations, in a letter to the magazine's editor.[60]

NOTES

1. Alfred C. Cordon letter to Leslie G. Arries, Jr., June 15, 1978, p. 1.

2. Cordon letter to Arries, September 22, 1978.

3. Taft Broadcasting Co., then the owner of WGR, on April 13, 1979, announced plans to build a $105 million amusement park and entertainment center near Toronto. Taft entered the venture with the Great-West Life Assurance Co. of Toronto. (See Courier-Express, "Amusement Park Plan Aired by Taft," April 13, 1979. See also, "Taft sees political light, eases border war stance," Toronto Star. October 20, 1979).

4. Cordon, September 22, 1978.

5. Cordon, July 10, 1978, p. 1.

6. House of Representatives Report 95-1684, 95th Congress, 2nd Session, October, 1978, p. 2.

7. Solomon, Hyman, "U.S. Bill Tries to Incite Fight Over Border TV," Financial Post, October 7, 1978, p. 10. See also "U.S. May Offer a Deal to Ease Convention Tax Law," Toronto Star, September 29, 1978, p. 460.

8. "A Confrontation with Canada Over TV Ads," Business Week, November 6, 1978, p. 142.

9. Six border stations filed an initial 301 complaint in November 1976, but it was not followed up. KVOS (Wotmeco) and WBEN were among the complainants; it makes a case similar to the case made in 1978. A somewhat similar brief also was filed on February 13, 1978, by ten border stations, including Taft and Capital Cities, in addition to WBEN and WIVB (formerly WBEN), to the Trade Policy Staff Committee, Office of the Special Representative for Trade Negotiations on concerns of U.S. service industries that were sought to be raised in the Multi-national Trade Negotiations (MTN). Repeal of Bill C-58 was sought.

10. Cordon, July 10, 1978, p. 3.

11. The submission was made on behalf of the following U.S. television licensees: KVOS Television Corporation Wotmeco, licensee of station KVOS Bellingham; Buffalo Broadcasting Co., licensee of station WIVB (formerly WBEN),

Buffalo; WPBN and WTOM, DBA Midwestern Television Company, licensee of station WPBN, Traverse City, Michigan; WPBN and WTOM DBA Midwestern Television Company, licensee of station WTOM, Cheyboygan, Michigan; Eastern Maine Broadcasting System, licensee of station WVII, Bangor, Maine; WDAY, licensee of station WDAZ, Grand Forks-Devils Lake, North Dakota; Great Lakes Television Co., licensee of station WSEE, Erie, Pennsylvania; Johnson Newspaper Corporation (formerly known as the Brockway Company), licensee of station WENY, Watertown, Spokane TV, licensee of station KZLY, Spokane, Washington; Spokane TV, licensee of station WTHI, Fargo, North Dakota; KMOS-TC, Inc., licensee of station DCFW, Kalispell, Montana; Advance Corporation, licensee of stations DFBB, Great Falls, Montana; and International Television Corporation, licensee of station WEZF, Burlington, Vermont.

12. Press release prepared by the border stations' public relations firm in Washington, Hill and Knowlton, Inc., August 29, 1978, p. 1.

13. Section 301(2) of the Trade Act of 1974, 10 USC 2411; Senate Finance Committee Report of the Trade Act of 1974, Senate Report no. 93-1298, 93rd Congress, 2nd Session, 165.

14. Hill and Knowlton, a Washington public relations firm, had appointments scheduled in Canada for Arries, Wolfson, and Fisher for August 30, 1978 as follows: 9:30 a.m., Blaik Kirby, radio and TV columnist, Globe and Mail; 11:00 a.m., Robert Duffy, acting head of the editorial page, Toronto Star; 12:30 p.m. (luncheon) with Robert MacDonald, columnist of the Toronto Sun, and Sheri Craig, radio and TV columnist of Marketing, 2:30 p.m., Margaret Laws, radio and TV coverage for the Financial Post.

15. Complaint filed pursuant to Section 301 of the Trade Act of 1974 before the Section 301 Committee of the Office of the Special Representative for Trade Negotiations, Washington, D.C., August 29, 1978, p. 4.

16. Ibid., pp. 5-8.

17. Violations of Article III, paragraphs 1, 2, and 4, as well as Article IV, were charged. They deal with equitability of taxes on imported and domestic products.

18. Brief filed in support of a complaint under Section 301 of the Trade Act of 1974 before the Section 301 Committee Office of the Special Representative for Trade Negotiations, November 22, 1978, pp. 55-73.

19. The existing income tax treaty between United States and Canada was signed March 4, 1942, and was supplemented by conventions signed August 8, 1956, and October 25, 1966.

20. Bart Fisher, intraborder stations' counsel, letter, February 23, 1978, p. 7.

21. The 301 panel chairman was Richard Rivers, general counsel, Office of the Special Representative for Trade Negotiations, assisted by Thomas Graham, deputy general counsel, Office of the Special Representative for Trade Negotiations. Other members of the panel were: Judy Davis, Commerce Department; Meyer Berstein, Labor Department; David Patterson, State Economic Bureau Department; and James Murphy, Treasury Department.

22. Witnesses for the U.S. broadcasters at the Section 301 hearing included: National Association of Broadcasters statement by Leslie G. Arries, Jr., member of the television board of directors of NAB and president of Buffalo Broadcasting Co., licensee of station WIVB, Buffalo; Richard F. Wolfson, executive vice president and

general counsel Wotmeco Enterprises; David Mintz, vice president and general manager, KVOS Television Corporation, licensee of station KVOS, Bellingham; and Bart Fisher of the law firm Patton, Boggs & Blow, border stations' counsel.

Witnesses for Canada's position included Canadian broadcasting stations: J. Ronald Mitchell, Moffat Communications, Winnipeg; Moses Znaimer, CITY-TV, Toronto; Donald Smith, CHAN-TV, Vancouver.

Witnesses for Canadian cable companies from Rogers Cable: Edward S. Rogers, president; Philip B. Lind, vice president; and J. S. Grafstein, queen's counsel, attorney from Minden, Gross, Grafstein & Greenstein, Toronto.

23. "Ottawa Uses its Weight in TV Ad War," Victoria (BC) Colonialist, November 29, 1978, p. 7.

24. Ibid.

25. Statement of the Canadian government's position concerning complaint of U.S. television licensees section relating to Section 19 of the Canadian Income Tax Act, November 29, 1978. See also rebuttal to a complaint made under Section 301 of the Trade Act of 1974 to the Section 301 Committee of the Office of the Special Trade Representative for Trade Negotiations, Washington, D.C., by J. S. Grafstein, counsel on behalf of Rogers Cable TV, December, 1978; statement of Jerry Grafstein, queen's counsel, Rogers Cable TV, Ltd., Toronto, before 301 Committee Office of the Special Representative for Trade Negotiations, November 28, 1978; outline of a submission to the Section 301 Committee of the Special Representative for Trade Negotiations, Washington, D.C., November 23, 1978.

26. Alfred C. Cordon, border stations' counsel, letter to Robert Howard, president of Howard Publications, owners of WIVB (formerly WBEN), December 1, 1978, p. 1.

27. Statement, p. 6.

28. Ibid.

29. Lawrence Martin, "Block Canadian Shows, U.S. Urged," Globe and Mail, November 30, 1978, p. 10.

30. Ibid.

31. Statement, pp. 6-9.

32. In the matter of complaint of KVOS Television Corp. et al. against Section 19 of the Canadian Income Tax Act (Bill C-58). Rebuttal brief before the Section 301 Committee of the Office of the Special Representative for Trade Negotiation, submitted by J. Ronald Mitchell, president and chief executive officers of Moffat Communications, Winnipeg, Manitoba; Moses Znaimer, president of CITY-TV, Toronto; and Donald M. Smith, executive vice president of CHAN-TV, Vancouver, British Columbia, 1978.

33. Ibid., p. 7.

34. Ibid.

35. Ibid.

36. Ibid., p. 15.

37. Edward S. Rogers, president of Rogers Cable TV, Toronto, statement before Section 301 Committee Office of the Special Representative for Trade Negotiations, November 29, 1978, pp. 6-7.

38. Outline, p. 4.

39. Ibid., p. 2.

40. Statement, p. 17.

41. Rogers, p. 6.

42. Those supporting the complaint but preferring negotiation to retaliation were: Taft Broadcasting Co., licensee of WGR, Buffalo; Capital Cities Communications, licensee of WKBW, Buffalo; Mt. Mansfield Television, licensee of WCAX, Burlington, New York; Rollins Telecasting, licensee of WPTZ, North Pole, New York; Aroostook Broadcasting Corporation, licensee of WAGM, Presque Isle, Maine; Community Broadcasting Services, licensee of WABI, Bangor, Maine; Great Lakes Communications, licensee of WICU, Pennsylvania; and RJR Communications, licensee of KBJR, Superior, Wisconsin.

43. Comments of certain U.S. Border Stations, in the matter of the petition by certain U.S. television licenses alleging certain unfair trade practices by the government of Canada, before the Section 301 Committee, Office of the Special Representatives for Trade Negotiations, November 29, 1978, p. 2.

44. Ibid., p. 10.

45. Ibid., p. 11.

46. The U.S. National Association of Broadcasters (NAB) is a non-profit incorporated association of radio and television stations whose membership, as of November 22, 1978, included 562 television stations, the national commercial networks, and 4,592 radio stations.   NAB opposed Bill C-58 in 1975, and the NAB executive committee reaffirmed the continuing opposition on November 17, 1978. NAB statement was presented by Leslie G. Arries, Jr., a member of the television board of directors of NAB, as well as president of WIVB, Buffalo (formerly WBEN).

47. Statement of NAB before the Section 301 Committee, Office of the Special Representative for Trade Negotiations, November 29, 1978.

48. The Canadian-U.S. Television Agreement of 1952, 2 UST(3)TIAS 2594; working arrangement for the allocation of VHF stations under the Canadian-U.S. TV Agreement of 1952, FCC Public Notice 2700 on March 29, 1961.   Under the agreement, the two countries entered into regional arrangements by which they agreed to an allocation of television frequencies, various principles governing their assignment and use, and a set of particular stations assignments.

49. Statement.

50. Ibid.

51. Ibid., p. 6.

52. Ibid., p. 7.

53. Barbara Keddy, "U.S. Border Stations Fight Hard to Regain Canadian TV Business," Globe and Mail, November 30, 1978, p. 11.

54. Tom Meser, "Sauve Stands Firm," Marketing, September 11, 1978, p. 12.

55. CBC-Radio Script, "As It Happens," 6:30 p.m. November 30, 1978.

56. Editorial, Toronto Star, "Use the Money to Improve TV," September 7, 1978, p. A8.

57. Editorial, Vancouver Sun, "Commerce and Culture," September 9, 1978, p. 4A.

58. Editorial, Broadcasting, "Coping with Canada," September 4, 1978, p. 66.

59. Ibid.

60. Editorial in Broadcasting brought a stinging letter to the editor from counsel to fourteen of the border stations. The attorneys told editor Sol Taishoff that "the Canadian government's new nationalism is one thing but the Canadians themselves have made it crystal clear that they want American television programs--

whether or not it erodes Canadian nationalism." They argued that Section 301 was very much realistic. "We can't conceive of greater realism," they stated, asking rhetorically, "When a violation has occurred, should business in the United States sit on its hands and not attempt to utilize a remedy which Congress has provided?" (see Taishoff letter regarding an editorial from counsel to fourteen border stations, September 12, 1978.)

6
Pulling It Together

As 1978 drew to a close, the border stations hoped to draw support from a special committee set up in Canada "to produce specific recommendations on a strategy to restructure the Canadian telecommunications system to contribute more effectively to the safeguarding of Canada's sovereignty."[1] The group, the Consultative Committee on the Implications of Telecommunications for Canadian Sovereignty, was to be known as the Clyne Committee, after its chairman, John V. Clyne.[2]

A border stations' memorandum indicated that in late December 1978, a representative of the border stations in Ottawa met with a Canadian senator, George Van Roggen, to review the border broadcasting dispute in depth. The representative, Thomas d'Aquino, asked Van Roggen to "intercede in our [the border stations'] behalf" with Clyne.[3]

d'Aquino stated:

> Last night [December 27, 1978] Senator Van Roggen called me to say that he had briefed Clyne at length on the C-58 problem, including foreign conventions linkage issue. The exercise was a valuable one in that Clyne apparently did not have an understanding of the history nor the issues in the border broadcasting dispute. As a result of the meeting, Senator Van Roggen has advised me that Clyne wishes to meet with representatives of the United States border stations in camera. Clyne is to call me to request the meeting.[4]

Ultimately, nine representatives of the U.S. border stations were to meet with the Clyne Committee.[5]

The Clyne Committee's recommendations were published in March 1979 and included moral support, at least, for the border stations' position. The Clyne Committee reported:

There is something repugnant to us in the notion that, whatever the legal niceties, it is permissible to pick up someone else's property off the air and tamper with it for profit. In this regard we think the U.S. border stations have cause to believe they are being unfairly treated. By saying this, we do not mean to support the case they are making for remedial action: what has happened is that they have been deprived, in one way or another, of part of the commercial value of what they regard as their property.[6]

Nonetheless, the Clyne Committee said it "did not feel moved" to recommend any change in the sense of Bill C-58. It did, however, recommend that the federal government should renew the discussions with the United States with a view of resolving the border television dispute at an early date.[7]

TRADE ACT REVISED

Meanwhile, before the Section 301 Committee could consider the border broadcasters' case on its merits, the committee needed to decide whether it had jurisdiction. Seeing the jurisdiction as only a "preliminary decision" to be resolved, the border stations' counsel was optimistic on the outcome of the case in February 1979.[8] The Section 301 Committee was greatly aided by congressional and administrative actions to amend the trade act to include broadcasting advertising. Two congressional committees approved including broadcasting amendments to the trade act: The senate's Finance Committee on March 15 recommended modification of Section 301 to indicate that the word "services" include broadcasting services in international trade.[9] Three weeks later, on April 5, the House's subcommittee on Ways and Means accepted the Finance Committee's recommendation.[10]

Amid the growing political atmosphere in the United States during this period of a policy of reciprocity with regard to Canada,[11] the trade act was quickly amended in the Spring of 1979 to ensure that broadcasting was covered; both houses of Congress, in consultation with the administration, recommended language to clarify Section 301 of the trade act:

According to the border stations:

This amending language removed any legal argument as to the applicability of the Trade Act protections in regard to border broadcast advertising service. This language was proposed and accepted specifically to answer Canadian arguments that Section 301 trade relief did not extend to the broadcasting industry.[12]

Under the revised Trade Act of 1979, jurisdiction for the 301 Committee was assured, and U.S. ambassador Alan Wolff, deputy special representative for trade negotiations, on June 1 sent a letter to the government of Canada indicating that jurisdiction had been found in favor of the border stations and that the Section 301 committee was proceeding to consider the case against Bill C-58 on its merits.[13] In addition, Wolff called on the government of Canada to enter into serious negotiations on Bill C-58 within thirty days; Canada, in response, requested a meeting in mid-July or early August.[14] Consultations were subsequently scheduled for August 15 on Bill C-58 and related matters.

The border stations' Section 301 complaint, the Clyne Committee's recommendation for talks, and an impending change of Prime Ministers in Canada appeared to have opened the door for talks.

Counsel for the border stations reflected: "We have had to laboriously pull the Canadians to the negotiation table . . . but it is clear now that we have arrived at a point where we will no longer get brushed off with the concept that C-58 is not negotiable."[15]

CANADIAN POLITICAL SHIFT

However, through the spring of 1979, Prime Minister Trudeau remained adamant that his country's elimination of Bill C-58 was an internal matter and not subject to negotiation, according to Senator Moynihan, who had talked with him on the issue.[16] But by the summer of 1979, Trudeau's eleven year reign was to end--temporarily as it turned out--and Joe Clark, a progressive conservative, took office June 4 as Canada's sixteenth and youngest prime minister.

A border broadcasters' strategy paper prepared shortly after Clark took office expressed "guarded optimism" that Canada's position might now change.[17] The prognosis was based on the fact that the Conservatives, at the time of Bill C-58's passage, had opposed the legislation on the basis that Bill C-58 was an inappropriate and counter productive means of achieving an otherwise laudable objective. The memorandum cautioned, however:

> Even so, this opposition should not be overemphasized as foretelling any great zeal by the new government in re-opening the C-58 issue if for no other reason than, while the conservatives opposed C-58, they did so in the context of the legislation per se and not the objective.[18]

FORMAL TALKS

Representatives of the governments of Canada and the United States met in Ottawa on August 15, 1979, on the Bill C-58 issue.[19] One of the principle results of the meeting was that the border stations now viewed Canada as willing to assess the issue: There was an "open window." Alfred Cordon, counsel for the border stations, commented:

> All in all, I believe that even though those at the meeting on the Canadian side were the same bureaucrats who were discussing or rather refusing to discuss this problem when Trudeau was around, there is a sincere desire to discuss this. The State Department refers to the co-called open window. As you very well know, there has been no open window heretofore.[20]

According to a joint communique issued at the conclusion of the meeting, the principle tangible step was a consensus to seek an industry-to-industry meeting; that is, the U.S. broadcasters would meet with the Canadian broadcasters to develop proposals for a resolution to the dispute, to be considered by the respective governments. The border stations subsequently sought to set up a meeting between NAB and CAB to develop a proposed solution.[21]

The U.S. border stations initially considered two proposals: that a fund be set up in Canada to strengthen Canadian broadcasting, and that each border station establish a taxable subsidiary or division in Canada that would pay Canadian taxes. The latter proposal was dropped, however, in response to Canadian concerns that the result might be to artificially encourage the establishment of a large number of new local Canadian sale arms for the border stations, and that the ordinary Canadian income taxes paid by such subsidiaries would not go directly to the benefit of the Canadian broadcaster system.[22]

FUND PROPOSED

Rather, the border stations suggested that they allocate 20 percent of the cross-border advertising revenue of U.S. border stations, after Canadian advertising agency fees, to support and strengthen the Canadian broadcast system. For example, under this plan, if the total revenue amounted to $20 million, this would produce an annual allocation to Canadian broadcasting of $3.5 million. It was envisioned that the funds would be deposited in a trust with a Canadian trust company. The trustees of the fund, through the U.S. border stations, would appoint a Canadian management company to administer and place investments from the fund into high-quality Canadian television programming. The Canadian management company would have 100 percent Canadian equity ownership with the Canadian board of directors, paying all taxes to the Canadian government.[23]

In return, Canada would agree to exempt the U.S. border stations from Bill C-58.   Implementation of the agreement was foreseen with the tax treaty negotiations still underway.

The proposal was agreed to by seventeen border stations, including the three in Buffalo and the station in Bellingham, and submitted to the Office of Canadian Affairs, U.S. State Department on October 12, 1979.

The border stations believed that the political climate within which this border proposal was being presented was favorable. The Conservative government was coalescing its power and was viewed as more amenable to a border broadcasting solution than the previous Liberal government because the proposal, the border stations felt, would appeal to the free enterprise stance of the Conservative government. It represented a private sector solution, which seemed to be the hoped-for thrust of the intergovernmental meeting in August.[24]

MAINTAIN PRESSURE

The border broadcasters, meanwhile, were maintaining pressure on Canada by continuing to block passage in Congress of easing restrictions affecting Canadian tourism. In the spring of 1979, the Senate Finance Committee held hearings on the Canadian exemption to the foreign conventions rule.   Senator Javits, in testimony before the committee, and Senator Moynihan, a member of the committee, opposed the exemption as long as Canada continued Bill C-58 in effect.

The lack of the Canadian tourism exemption was costing Canada $100 million a year, according a Reginald K. Groome, an official of the Tourism Industry Association of Canada.[25] Groome, the association's vice chairman, complained bitterly in a speech in Canada that the Canadian restriction had caused a "major loss in Canada jobs" and hurt U.S. interests too. He noted that many of Canada's convention hotels were American owned and operated; the hotel workers' union was headquartered in New York, and more than half of the airlines providing service for U.S. conventioners were American owned, as were the car rental and sightseeing companies. Declaring that there "seems to be little doubt" that reform of the U.S. law granting Canada an exemption has been linked to the abolition or modification of Bill C-58, Groome asserted:

One is inclined to agree that Canada and, more specifically, its tourist industry, is literally being held for ransom through the linkage process, that we are being blackmailed. For tourism is a hostage and innocent victim in this war of linkage.[26]

Groome attacked the varied Canadian and American interests of Wotmeco, corporate owners of KVOS in Bellingham, which operates television stations, motion picture theaters, soft drink bottling companies, and tourist attractions in North America. He stated that Wotmeco's broadcast division performance overall, despite the impact on the one station, KVOS, can "only be described as heart-rending--a mere 71 percent increase in division profits on a 49 percent increase in sales." Groome wondered out loud if the "bartering process" advocated by Wotmeco and other border broadcasters suggests a similar course of action for Canadians:

> For example, should British Columbians boycott Coca-Cola products produced by Wotmeco in Vancouver, Chilliwach and Vernon until such time as Wotmeco drops its opposition to reform of Section 602 [of the Tax Reform Act of 1976]? Should Newfoundlanders boycott Coca-Cola products produced by Wotmeco in St. John's Bishop's Falls and Corner Book, Newfoundland?   In even broader terms, should Canadians visiting Florida make a point of boycotting the Miami Seaquarium because it belongs to Wotmeco and because Wotmeco is among those hurting Canada and the Canadians? Should Canadian vacationers boycott Wotmeco's 38 cinemas dotting Florida?   Their vending operations in Florida?   Should Canadians shun Wotmeco's 45 cinemas when they visit Puerto Rico, the Dominican Republic, the Bahamas and the Virgin Islands?[27]

CONTACT CARTER

Late in 1979, the border broadcasters sought to make sure President Carter would bring up the border broadcast issue in a planned November 9 meeting with Canada's new prime minister, Joe Clark. Alfred Cordon noted how that was handled:

> We had concerns as to whether or not the President would bring up the border television problem with Prime Minister Clark. Our meetings with the State Department led us to believe that the President's briefing book would have the full story on the Canadian problem; but there was a question as to whether or not he would actually bring it up.[28]

For insurance, contact was made with a legislative aide to Senator Moynihan with whom Leslie Arries had a close association; it was ultimately agreed that Moynihan would discuss the broadcast issue with the president and provide him with a letter concerning the issue. Moynihan subsequently was reported to have contacted Carter late in the afternoon prior to his departure to Canada, and he discussed the border broadcast problem with him "quite extensively" and gave him the letter.[29] Moynihan's letter recalled the Senate's resolution that the President raise the issue with Canada. Moynihan emphasized:

> That the problems extend well beyond the issue of the revenue lost or gained by American broadcasters. What is at stake is the continued health and strength of U.S.-Canadian relations; relations, moreover, which are critical to the well-being of the entire North American continent.[30]

The president and Clark, however, did not meet as planned, as the session was postponed due to circumstances that arose in the Iranian hostage crisis.

As 1979 drew to a close, the border stations sought to maintain what they viewed as significant momentum towards effective use of what was termed the "open window" with the Canadian government. The border stations' governmental advisors in Ottawa believed that the awareness of the dispute by the government of Canada had "increased very considerably" such that "some discernible progress" had been recorded with the Progressive Conservative government of Clark. A "reluctant willingness" was seen on the part of the Canadian government to recognize the "high irritation factor" of the dispute in bilateral terms. The advisor suggested that the border stations must maintain unity and "launch a fresh campaign" in the first half of 1980.[31]

TAX TREATY LEVERAGE

As the 1980's began, however, border broadcasters were losing their leverage with regard to a new tax treaty being negotiated by Canada and the United States. The update of the 1942 agreement, under renegotiation for the last seven years, was reportedly to trade off the border broadcast opposition to the Canadian tourist exemption for "bigger issues," according to counsel for the border stations.[32] What the bigger issues were, however, were not known at that point-- mid-March, 1980. In letters to senators Javits and Moynihan, Arries warned of "recent and disturbing events within the Department of Treasury which risk a serious setback in our joint efforts to solve" the dispute.[33] Arries indicated that it was understood that staff-level agreements were made-- but had not yet submitted to policy-level officials--to the effect that: Treasury may have agreed to give the Canadians relief from foreign conventions travel restrictions without any Canadian concessions to Bill C-58, and thereby undercut the position of the House and Senate linking the two issues."[34]

Javits replied on March 27, 1980, that U.S. negotiations "made no specific commitments" but that, in an effort to "break the impasse," did attempt to determine what Canada would be prepared to offer in return for convention tax relief.[35]

The Treasury Department, however, pursued negotiations along the lines of trading off the border issue for a reduction to U.S. citizens on taxes for dividends and royalties from 15 to 10 percent, counsel records show, and, on May 23, 1980, Canada announced in a press release that an agreement on a tax treaty had been reached with the United States.[36] Donald Lubick, assistant U.S. treasury secretary for tax policy, confirmed the tentative pact before the U.S. Senate Finance Committee session on the foreign convention exemption issue; he said the treaty was under review by the State Department and the White House. Lubick added that U.S. negotiators had fought hard on the issue of allowing deductions for Canadian advertisers on U.S. border stations but that the Canadian government would not budge.[37] The Treasury Department did agree to defer announcing the treaty after a meeting with representatives of the border broadcasters.

The senate committee decided to postpone action on the tourist exemption until at least mid-August 1980, to allow time for the President to make a decision on the Section 301 complaint. In September 1980, the Treasury Department announced signing the tax treaty. Section XXV(9) exempted Canada from the foreign convention restrictions, and expenses in Canada were to be deductible to the same extent they would be if the convention were held in the United States. Bill C-58, however, remained in place. In November 1980, Carter submitted the tax treaty to the Senate for ratification.

JOINT MEETING

Plans also were underway for a broadcast industry-to-industry meeting between the associations of both countries, as recommended at the intergovernmental conference on August 15, 1979. Representatives of the two nations' over-the-air broadcast organizations--CAB and NAB--met April 21, 1980, in Toronto.[38] Agencies of both governments had indicated in the August meeting that the terms of the solution of this dispute would be best settled between the broadcasters of the two countries. Such a solution was seen more likely to be directly related to the issues, more easily understood by both parties, in keeping with private sector goals and objectives, and leading to further cooperation between the broadcasters of both countries on bigger issues in the future.[39]

Leslie Arries told the Canadian broadcasters that the alternative from the U.S. broadcasters' viewpoint was a government-mandated solution that may be unrealistic, unfair, and cause additional paperwork and government control. Further, not reaching some agreement was seen as costing additional time and money in legal fees, meetings, research, and perhaps permanent roadblocks to cross-border communication.[40]

Another consideration the border stations had was that technology at the beginning of the 1980's indicated that the border stations could be made superfluous as a signal source in Canada since satellite-to-home communications could be achieved by both countries.

The border stations warned that if Canada chose to leapfrog border stations--that is, receive U.S. signals from American stations farther south of the border that lack an incentive to sell in Canadian markets--the end process would be detrimental to both countries' over-the-air broadcast industries.[41] "Super stations" distributed by satellite throughout Canada, the border stations argued, would be "hostile to the interests" of both countries' over-the-air industries and "destructive of fair and orderly competition" on both sides of the border.[42]

Discounting dual licensing (U.S. and Canadian stations) because neither the U.S. nor Canadian law would permit it, the border broadcasters reiterated their proposal for a production fund but noted it was understood the proposal had been regarded as "unacceptable" to Canada.[43] Arries indicated the proposal of a contribution and a tax presence were characterized as "insulting" by the Canadian broadcasters and caused the "thorniest" period.[44] Summarizing the session, Arries contended: "In my opinion, and I feel sure in the opinion of the other U.S. broadcasters, it's impossible to resolve the border broadcast issue with Canadian broadcasters or even to be able to offer suggested solutions to governments."[45]

The two broadcast associations, in a joint statement following the meeting, termed the talks "amicable" and reiterated the two sides' historic--and polar--positions. The statement added that both sides felt there was a responsibility for cable "to share its success with those whose signals it used."[46]

301 PROSPECTS GOOD

By mid-May of 1980, border station counsel believed the Section 301 Committee was going to rule in favor of the border broadcasters -- that there would be a finding against Canada for carrying on an unfair trade practice.[47] However, while awaiting the announcement, the border stations' attorneys proposed "to send a message across the border." It would take two forms: having a "number of Senators prominent in the dispute" sign a letter to Ambassador Reubin Askew of the Office of the Special Trade Representative, pointing out Congress's concern to link relief of the Canadian tourism exemption and the border broadcaster issues, and setting up a colloquy on the floor of the Senate among some nine Senators to press the linkage concept. Counsel for the border stations even provided drafts of separate, but coordinated, statements for each senator.

The border stations also requested another hearing before the Section 301 Committee, and the U.S. Trade representative scheduled July 9, 1980, for presentations regarding measures towards Canada.[48] In a brief, the 14 border stations suggested that the President take a number of retaliatory actions: special duties, or quantitative restrictions, on exports of Canadian feature films and records to the United States; support of U.S. legislation that would be a mirror image of Canada's Bill C-58 (that is, tax legislation which that preclude U.S. taxpayers from deducting the costs of advertising on Canadian television and radio); continue to deny Canada special relief from the U.S. tax law, which limits expense deductions for attending foreign conventions; and adopt a policy that would require consideration of the unreasonable nature of Bill C-58 in other matters of Canadian-U.S. concerns (i.e., linkage and reciprocity), such as allocation of fishing rights.[49]

Senator Moynihan, Senator Heinz, NAB, and executives and attorneys for the border stations testified in support of the retaliation measures. CAB opposed it. Moynihan urged continuing efforts to link the broadcasting issue to foreign convention tax relief and warned that the Senate would take "a long, hard look" when the tax treaty came to the Senate for approval.[50]   Heinz, whose constituency includes a station in Erie, Pennsylvania, hard hit by Bill C-58, noted that Canada appears to be pursuing a policy of economic nationalism.[51] He added: "Our primary sentiment is one of outrage -- outrage that Canada permits the piracy of U.S. programming without compensation and hopes Congress will grant an . . . exemption . . . dealing with the deductibility of foreign conventions."[52]

Arries noted that he came home from the Toronto meeting between the NAB and CAB "convinced that it is impossible to resolve the border broadcast issue solely within the private sector."[53]   He urged the resolution on a government-to-government basis, through the Section 301 complaint.

An attorney for the border stations, Sheldon S. Cohen, proposed the mirror legislation, which would amend the U.S. Internal Revenue Code to deny a U.S. income tax deduction for the cost of advertising placed by American firms on a Canadian station.[54] Two Canadian broadcast stations--a television station and a radio station--received "considerable advertising revenues" from the Detroit market, according to Cohen and the border stations' brief.[55]   CBET-TV of Windsor, Ontario, and radio station CKLW, also of Windsor, both broadcast to the Detroit market. The owner of CKLW, John Bassett, in 1974 testimony before the CRTC said that 93 percent of the station's revenue came from U.S. advertising directed at the Detroit, Cleveland, and Akron markets.[56]

CANADIAN "CANDY"

CAB and three Canadian stations contended that the border stations, having tasted the Canadian "candy" for so long, simply refused to recognize that they had no legal right to it.[57] CAB contested references by Arries and Wotmeco's Richard Wolfson, concerning the Canadian-U.S. Television Agreement of 1952. CAB noted that, under the agreement, Buffalo stations' signal protection does not extend to Toronto but falls eight miles short. All the agreement does, CAB argued, is ensure Canada would not interfere with U.S. stations' signals within the United States, and that the United States would not interfere with Canadian stations' signals within Canada. The pact, in effect, does not, in itself, allow the Toronto market for the Buffalo stations, according to the CAB position.[58]

NOTES

1. Canadian Department of Communications, news release, "Independent Committee to Recommend on the Future of Telecommunications in Canada," November, 1978, p. 1.

2. John V. Clyne of Vancouver, British Columbia, was chancellor of the University of British Columbia. He was formerly chairman of the board of MacMillan Bloedel and was from 1950-57, a justice of the supreme court of British Columbia. He had served as sole royal commissioner in three public inquiries.

3. Thomas d'Aquino was a member of Intercounsel in Ottawa, advisors to the Canadian government on policy, legislation and operations. The firm represented the U.S. border stations.

4. Thomas d'Aquino, Intercounsel, Ottawa, "Memorandum re: Consultative Committee on the Implications of Telecommunications for Canadian Sovereignty," December 28, 1978, p. 1.

5. The following delegates from U.S. border television stations were received by the Clyne Committee: Richard F. Wolfson, executive vice president and general counsel of Wotmeco Enterprises, owner KVOS Television Corp., licensee KVOS, Bellingham; Leslie G. Arries, Jr., president of Buffalo Broadcasting Company, licensee WIVB, Buffalo; Charles Goodell, attorney of Capital Cities Communications, Buffalo, licensee WKBW, Buffalo; David Mintz, vice president and general manager of KVOS, Bellingham; John Fiorini, III, counsel of Smith & Pepper, Washington, D.C.; Allan R. O'Brien, counsel of Gowling & Henderson, Ottawa, Ontario; Thomas d'Aquino, consultant for Intercounsel, Ottawa, Ontario; C. Gaylord Watkins, associate counsel for Hewitt, Hewitt, Nesbitt, & Reid, Ottawa, Ontario. See Clyne Committee, J. V. Clyne, chairman of the Consultative Committee on the Implications of Telecommunications for Canadian Sovereignty, which prepared Telecommunications and Canada, Hull, Quebec: Canadian Government Publishing Center, Supply and Services, March 1979, p. 94.

6. Clyne Committee, J. V. Clyne, chairman of the Consultative Committee on the Implications of Telecommunications for Canadian Sovereignty, which prepared Telecommunications and Canada, Hull, Quebec: Canadian Government Publishing Center, Supply and Services, March 1979, p. 42.

7. Ibid., p. 46.

8. Bart Fisher, counsel for border stations, letter, May 4, 1979.

9. Senate Finance Committee press release No. 108, March, 1979, p. 4.

10. House Subcommittee on Trade, Committee on Ways and Means press release no. 17, April, 1979, p. 1.

11. Stephen Clarkson, Canada and the Reagan Challenge: Crisis in Canadian-American Relationship, (Toronto: James Lorimer & Co., 1982).

12. Briefing Book, U.S.-Canadian Border Broadcasting Dispute, prepared by border stations' counsel, December, 1980.

13. Marcus Cohen, letter from border station counsel to Robert S. Strauss, U.S. Special Representative for trade negotiations, July 12, 1979, p. 1.

14. Ibid., pp. 1-2.

15. Alfred C. Cordon, border stations' counsel, in letter to Leslie G. Arries, Jr., president, WIVB, Buffalo, July 10, 1979, pp. 1-2.

16. Roland Powell, "Canada Bars Talks on Tax Deduction for U.S. TV Ads," Buffalo Evening News, March 14, 1979, p. 40.

17. Memorandum: Bill C-58, Strategy, prepared by A. R. O'Brien, counsel for border stations, June 21, 1979, p. 2.

18. Ibid.

19. The U.S. representatives included Richard Smith, director of the Canada Desk, State Department, and Robert Jamerschlag, Canadian affairs negotiator, Office of the Special Representative for trade negotiations. Representatives from Canada at the negotiations included Russ McKinney, director general of the Bureau of U.S. Affairs, Ministry of External Affairs.

20. Cordon, August 23, 1979, p. 2.

21. Canada-U.S. discussions on border broadcasting, "Notes for Use in Response to Media Enquiries", Communique made available following intergovernmental meeting, August 15, 1979.

22. "Border Broadcasting Negotiation Positions, discussion paper submitted to the U.S. State Department, October 12, 1979, p. 1.

23. Proposed solution to Canadian-U.S. border broadcast dispute, executional paper, prepared by border stations' counsel, November 15, 1979, p. 5.

24. Ibid., p. 1.

25. Reginald K. Groome, vice chairman of the Tourism Industry Association of Canada, "An Eye for an Eye or a Neighborly Response," speech on Travel and Tourism Day of the Canadian National Exhibition Association, September 2, 1979, p.4.

26. Ibid., p. 5.

27. Ibid., p. 8.

28. Cordon, letter August 30, 1979, p.1.

29. Senator Daniel Moynihan, letter to President Carter, November 6, 1979, p. 1.

30. Ibid., p. 2.

31. Intercounsel, letter to Wotmeco, owners of KVOS, Bellingham, from Thomas d'Aquino of Intercounsel, Ottawa, December 28, 1979, p. 2.

32. Cordon, letter, March 13, 1980, p. 1.

33. Leslie G. Arries, Jr., letter to Senator Jacob Javits, March 17, 1980, p. 1. Similar to his letter to Moynihan, March 13.

34. Ibid., p. 2.

35. Senator Jacob Javits, letter to Leslie G. Arries, Jr., March 27, 1980.

36. Finance Department, Canada press release no. 80-37, May 23, 1980. Canadian finance minister Allan J. MacEachen announced the agreement reached between his department and the U.S. Treasury Department. It reduced by 5 percent the terms of the treatment of taxation of income and capital. The pact, subject to legislative approval in both the United States and Canada, provides that the maximum rates of withholding on taxes on nonresidents may not exceed 10 percent of direct dividends, patent royalties, and technical know-how payments, and 15 percent of portfolio dividends, interest, and periodic pension payments. Direct dividends include those paid to a company owning 10 percent or more of the voting stock of the company paying the dividend. Under the existing 1942 Treaty, the withholding tax rates on nonresidents are generally 15 percent. The pact also ensures that any profit or income from real property, including natural resource royalties, may be fully taxed in the country where the property is located.

37. "Taxation: Finance Committee Delays Foreign Convention Rule to give USTR Chance to Deal on Broadcasting Issue," U.S. Export Weekly, May 27, 1980.

38. Representatives at the meeting from Canada were: Ernest Steele, president of CAB; Don Smith, chairman of CAB; Jim Purvis, general manager of CKY-TV, Winnipeg; Don Brinton, president, CKND-TV, Winnipeg, Manitoba; Lee Hableton, general manager of CFCF-TV, Montreal; John Coleman, director, government and industry liaison of CTV, Toronto, Ontario; Moses Znaimer, president of CITY-TV, Toronto, Ontario; Alain Gourd, vice chairman of CAB; David Mintz, president of Global Television Network (formerly of KVOS of Bellingham); Don Mills, Ontario; Wayne Stacy, CAB. Representatives from the United States were: Leslie G. Arries, Jr., president of WIVB (formerly WBEN), Buffalo; Forest W. Amsden, vice president and general manager of KING-TV, Seattle; Philip R. Beuth, vice president and general manager of WKBW, Buffalo; Peter R. Martin, vice president, and news and public affairs director of WCAX, South Burlington, Vermont; and Richard F. Wolfson, executive vice president and general manager of Wotmeco Enterprises, Miami, Florida.

39. Statement by the U.S. Border Broadcasters' Committee, "The Importance of Our Meeting on the Border Broadcaster Dispute," April 12, 1980.

40. Ibid.

41. Some suggestions of common ground, "Statement for All Broadcasters Affected by the Canadian-U.S. Border Broadcasting Dispute," April 21, 1980, p. 5.

42. Ibid.

43. Ibid., p. 3.

44. Leslie G. Arries, Jr., letter to Robert J. King, senior vice president, Capital Cities Communication, April 24, 1980, p. 1.

45. Ibid.

46. Joint statement of CAB and NAB committees, on border broadcast issues, April 21, 1980.

47.   Alfred C. Cordon, letter to Robert Howard, president of   Howard Publications, owners of WIVB, May 21, 1980, p. 1.

48.   Federal Register, vol. 45, no. 122, June 23, 1980.

49.   Supplemental submission pertaining to appropriate relief, brief filed in support of complaint under Section 301 of the Trade Act of 1974, February 19, 1980.

50.   Senator Patrick Moynihan, testimony before the Section 301 Committee of the Office of the U.S. Trade Representative, July 29, 1980, pp. 1-3.

51.   Senator John Heinz, testimony before the Section 301 Committee of the U.S. Trade Representative, July 9, 1980, p. 2.

52.   Ibid.

53.   Leslie G. Arries, Jr., letter to Robert J. King, senior vice president of Capital Cities Communication, April 24, 1980, p. 5.

54.   Supplemental submission pertaining to appropriate relief, brief filed in support of complaint under Section 301 of the Trade Act of 1974, February 19, 1980, p. 102.

55.   Ibid., pp. 13-14.

56.   Ibid. Comprised of testimony before the Canadian Radio-television and Telecommunications Commission, "Proposed New Radio and Television Broadcasting Regulations, Canadian Production of Commercials," October 8, 1974.

57.   Rebuttal brief of CAB before Section 301 Committee of the Office of Special Representative for Trade Negotiations, Washington, D.C., by J. S. Grafstein, counsel on behalf of Rogers Cable TV, December 1980, p. 1.

58.   Ibid., pp. 9-12.

7

Some Battles Won/War Winds Down

The Section 301 Committee was required to make its recommendation to the President by July 26, 1980 (under a schedule set by the revised Trade Act of 1979), and it did so. However, the border stations were not able to confirm what the Section 301 recommendation was. On July 28, Alfred C. Cordon, counsel for WIVB (formerly WBEN), reported that one of the reasons for nondisclosure was to insulate the President from lobbyists:

> The 26th of July has come and gone, and we have learned that the 301 Committee has met and has made certain recommendations to the President. However, we are unable to find out what those recommendations were at the moment. The reason is that if the matter were made public, then the President might be subject to lobbying, which is probably true .... I cannot think that the recommendations would be other than along the line we have heretofore recommended to the committee. Whether all will be adopted, I cannot say.[1]

CARTER'S DECISION

On July 31, 1980, President Carter disclosed that he had found Canada guilty of a trade violation and asked Congress to pass a mirror bill; that is, a U.S. version of Bill C-58. Carter issued a memorandum that he had determined that Bill C-58 was "unreasonable" and "burdens and restricts" U.S. commerce, within the meaning of Section 301.[2] The president noted that consultations between the Canadian and U.S. governments, as well as broadcasters from two countries, failed to achieve a mutually acceptable solution that would address the Canadian culture objective without having an adverse impact on the U.S. broadcasting stations.   Thus, Carter said, the most appropriate response to the Canadian practice, Bill C-58, was to propose legislation in Congress, that when enacted, would mirror the Canadian practice.

Carter noted that such a measure is "most appropriate" because it is directed at those interests in Canada--broadcasters--that now benefit from the denial of Canadian advertising revenues to U.S. border broadcasters.

The President added a sunset provision. He concluded that the proposed law will apply only as long as the Canadian law, Bill C-58, applies.[3]

PARTIAL VICTORY

Reaction by the border stations' counsel was one of a sense of victory tempered by the reality that a mirror law was but one of the number of alternatives and perhaps the least damaging to Canada.

Cordon explained: "We understand that the 301 Committee considered all our requests for retaliation but could not get a unanimous vote except on the so-called mirror law . . . . In sum, we did win, although we did not win at all."[4]

The President's decision drew little enthusiasm from border station counsel in Ottawa. Allan R. O'Brien commented:

It [the President's response] is basically a political document; i.e., it responds to the findings of the Office of the U.S. Trade Representative in the least objectionable way to Canada. At the same time, the Office of the President can take the position that they acted promptly to the finding and adopted at least one of the recommendations of the petitioners.[5]

Nonetheless, this was the first time under Section 301 of the Trade Act that a decision had wound its way to the president and retaliation taken. Other complaints had been resolved in the process prior to reaching presidential action.[6]

Preliminary indications were, however, that the Canadian government did not intend to change its policy in regard to Bill C-58.[7] Cordon, appraised the situation:

Notwithstanding this reprisal is the most dramatic ever taken under Section 301, additional steps will have to be taken to affect Canada's policy on C-58. We will continue efforts in the Congress to maintain the existing linkage between relief for U.S. broadcasters from C-58 and relief for Canada from U.S. limitations on the deductibility of foreign convention

expenses . . . . Also we will take action to see that the Tax
Treaty is not signed.[8]

MIRROR LEGISLATION

Despite the border stations' rhetoric, for the next several years,
mirror legislation became the dominant thrust of the border stations'
campaign against Bill C-58, ultimately seeking to link it to blocking
importation of a new Canadian communications system--Telidon, a
videotex system.   Despite the border stations' effort to scuttle the
tourism exemption in Congress, it was approved on December 13,
1980, and the border stations lost a key bargaining chip.

Carter, on September 9, 1980, presented the first mirror law to
Congress and urged its early passage.[9]   The proposed mirror law
would affect two Canada stations and cost Canada nearly $5 million
annually in lost advertising, according to the Office of the U.S. Trade
Representative.[10]   CKLW-Radio in Windsor, Ontario, owned by
Toronto-based Baton Broadcasting, stood to lose most, if not all, of
the $3.5 million it was reported collecting from Detroit advertisers.[11]
CBET-TV, a CBC television station in Windsor, would lose $750,000
or one-half of its annual revenue.[12]   The television station's program
director said, however, that the station's rates were much lower than
those of Detroit stations, and he hoped his U.S. advertisers might still
find it profitable to continue to do business with CBET, even without
the tax deductibility.[13]   An advocate for CKLW, which gets up to 90
percent of its revenues from the Detroit market, said the station might
no longer be able to afford the high-priced American DJ's, or justify
the big Detroit sales office.   CKLW ratings in 1980 had shown 797,300
Americans and 215,500 Canadians tuning in.[14]

WEIGH APPROACH

As 1981 began, the United States had a new president, Ronald
Reagan, and Trudeau was back in office as prime minister of Canada.
The change led Bart S. Fisher, counsel for the border stations, to
suggest a direct approach: "When Reagan meets Trudeau . . . the first
words out of his mouth should be to bitch about Bill C-58."[15]

Despite the rhetoric, the border stations were reassessing
whether it would be feasible to bend Canada's resolve on Bill C-58.   In
mid-January 1981, representatives of Wotmeco were to meet in
Miami and decide its role in the next stage of the border war.   Fisher
analyzed the prospects prior to the session:

The bottom-line corporate question for Wotmeco is: Should
we spend any more money on the C-58 project, in light of the
foreign conventions reversal, and the less than adequate relief

from the 301 case? A corollary to this is: Could Wotmeco cut a separate deal in Canada, and avoid all the aggravation of a 'general' solution?[16]

Fisher answered his own question, stating that he believed that one more year should be spent on trying to reverse the Bill C-58 situation in Canada. He explained:

I would not have said that had Carter been re-elected, and the Congress remained as it was. But the Canadians have high hopes that Reagan will place the improvement of U.S.-Canadian relations near the top of his foreign policy agenda. If we can immediately demonstrate that the C-58 issue will remain as an irritant for the duration of the Reagan Administration, we might have a chance, although realistically, the possibilities for major C-58 reform under this scenario are slim.[17]

The result was that the border stations main method to move Canada on Bill C-58 became mirror legislation.[18]

REAGAN TOUGHENS STATEMENT

On November 17, 1981, Reagan sent a message to Congress urging mirror legislation. The message was similar to Carter's the year before, but tougher. Reagan added a warning:

I recognize, however, that this amendment by itself may not cause the Canadians to resolve the dispute. Therefore, I note that I retain the right to take further action, if appropriate, to obtain the elimination of the practice on my own motion under the authority of Section 301(c)(1). Hopefully, this will not be necessary.[19]

Responding to the Reagan message, Representative Barber Conable, Jr., introduced a bill on December 14, 1981, which would mirror Bill C-58 (HR 5205).[20] A similar bill (S 2051) was introduced in the Senate on February 2, 1982, by Senator John Danforth.[21] Before the House, Conable elevated the issue by tying it into the principle of free trade. He stated:

I would hope, however, that our friends in Canada understand that this measure reflects the commitment of the Congress and the President to the promotion of free trade, while at the same time insuring that our trade laws operate effectively to protect U.S. industry from unreasonable and restrictive practices.[22]

Danforth took a similar position introducing the mirror legislation:

The communication industry is one of our important service industries and the service sector is becoming an increasingly important growth area on our export ledger. Thus, it is vitally important that we reinforce one of the few legal mechanisms which U.S. service exporters can invoke to gain relief from foreign trade barriers.[23]

TELIDON AMENDMENT

In June of 1982, Senator Moynihan added an amendment to the proposed mirror legislation that would increase the dollar value of the U.S. retaliatory impact. The amendment would deny to U.S. businesses a tax deduction and tax credit for the purchase of Telidon, the Canadian videotex system. Moynihan noted that the prospective economic effect on Canada would be significant. The Canadians had predicted an annual U.S. market of $12 billion for videotex in the United States by 1990, and the Canadians hoped that their advanced and sought-after system would be able to account for $1 billion in that market.

In the spring of 1983, the border stations proposed to trade off the Telidon campaign if Canada would accept the latest proposal by the border stations'. The border stations asked Canada to adjust Bill C-58 so that 30 percent of their Canadian advertising would be subject to the bill but 70 percent exempt. The 30 percent figure, Arries explained, represented more than twice the penetration of the Canadian market by any border station.[24]

COMPROMISE SHORT-LIVED

Stations were cautiously optimistic that the new proposal might move Canada on Bill C-58. Accordingly, counsel for the border stations indicated that in response to "informal signals" from Canadian officials that negotiation might be possible, Congress took no action on the mirror bills; the Reagan administration did not immediately request reintroduction of the bills in the 98th Congress.

The optimism was short lived, however. A U.S. government delegation met with a Canadian delegation on March 16, 1983, but Canada, counsel reported, backed off:

The U.S. presented a proposal which the Canadians had indicated informally would be a reasonable approach. Since

then, the Canadians have backed off, commissioning a study
[a follow up to Donner and Lazar]."[25]

Once again, negotiation had not been fruitful. It was back to
retaliation. On August 3, 1983, William E. Brock, the U.S. trade
representative, asked George Bush, president of the Senate, to renew
congressional action on mirror legislation.[26] The bill was passed by
the Senate's Finance Committee on November 8, 1983.[27]
        Meanwhile, Canada remained, in principle, adamant on Bill C-
58. Canada was particularly irritated by the linkage to other issues,
spokespersons   in   External   Affairs   and   the   Department   of
Communication indicated, in separate interviews in 1983.[28]

MIRROR BILL ENACTED

        Ultimately, the border broadcasters lobbying efforts for mirror
legislation were successful. In the fall of 1984, Reagan signed an
omnibus trade bill that included a measure denying tax breaks with
Americans who advertise on Canadian stations that have American
audiences.[29]   The effect was limited largely to stations opposite
Detroit, in the Windsor, Ontario area. Canada did not, however,
amend Bill C-58, and the effort to link the Telidon curb to the mirror
bill was not successful.
        Following this retaliatory volley, negotiations were conducted
during talks on St. Patrick's Day, 1985, between Prime Minister
Mulroney and Reagan. A bilateral mechanism, an interagency group
from both sides, was established to help resolve trade barrier
problems, including the border dispute. During that session, the
border stations pressed for a three-year moratorium on Bill C-58.
Canada proposed to tax only half the advertising revenue place on
U.S. stations, if the border stations would stop lobbying. Neither
proposal was approved. Canada rejected the moratorium and the
U.S. television border stations refused to stop lobbying.[30]
        As the stakes, in terms of the advertising dollars retained in
Canada, mounted in the mid-1980's--nearly $40 million, or double the
$20 million figure of the mid-1970's--Canada remained adamant on
Bill C-58.[31] A national study in 1986 conceded that Bill C-58 hadn't
met its cultural objective but recommended that the bill remain in
place as economically vital to Canada. The Report of the Task Force
on Broadcasting Policy, referring to the fact that the stations
purchased more U.S. shows with the extra revenue rather than
produce more Canadian shows, noted that "much as we regret the
counter-productive impact on Canadian programming of Bill C-58
and simultaneous substitution, we endorse their maintenance. Their
legislative purpose is the protection of an orderly market based on the
property rights duly purchased and held by Canadian broadcasters."[32]

FREE-TRADE EFFORTS

By 1986, the border stations' efforts shifted to the free trade talks, through which both countries would seek an accord that would remove most trade and investment barriers.   Arries told a congressional hearing in the fall of 1986: "The negotiations for a free trade agreement now in progress present a definite opportunity for resolution of the border dispute that must not slip away . . .   If the negotiations are to be successful, they cannot ignore Bill C-58, but must establish a process for its elimination."[33]

Lobbying efforts were well underway by the summer of 1987. U.S. House Speaker Jim Wright wrote to Ambassador Clayton Yeutter, the U.S. trade representative, pressing for a resolution to the border broadcast dispute in the context of the Free Trade Agreement:

> Negotiations with Canada for an Agreement governing free trade between our countries are now in the final stages. In that regard, I want to reaffirm to you my interest that any such agreement contain a resolution of the border broadcast issue which has been an irritant in our trade relations. . . . Neither consultations nor the enactment of mirror legislation has resolved the problem. Your negotiations should.[34]

Eight U.S. senators sounded a similar theme in a letter to the trade representative:

> Your negotiations with the Government of Canada present an unprecedented opportunity to lay a foundation for expanded trade between our two countries that could benefit us both greatly. We look forward to seeing the results of your efforts and making our own judgments as to whether the proposed agreement is in the best interest of the United States. One criteria by which we will make that judgment is whether the proposed agreement resolves outstanding trade disputes. 'Border Broadcasting' is one of the oldest. It is long past time that Canada abandon its blatant protectionism in broadcasting.   Your negotiations present the perfect opportunity to achieve that result.[35]

NO C-58 RELIEF

In the beginning of 1988, the border stations explored participation in a joint effort by those seeking to defeat the proposed Free Trade Agreement. The group, the U.S./Canadian Free Trade Coalition, included representatives of the maritime industries, mining interests, auto parts suppliers, and nonferrous metals manufacturers.[36]

However, by the summer of 1988, the Free Trade Agreement had widespread support in the United States, and the border television stations had determined they couldn't hold the agreement "captive," as they had the convention tax relief exemption.[37] Ultimately signed by President Reagan and Prime Minister Mulroney, the agreement, confirmed by both countries' legislatures, doesn't contain any direct Bill C-58 advertising relief for the border broadcasters.[38]

WAR WINDS DOWN

By the summer of 1988 the war had wound down, with only an "occasional skirmish" foreseen, according to Arries.[39] His station in 1988 had just changed owners. He explained several reasons for the war's winding down. First, it wasn't that the border stations were "not willing to fight," but that it was "difficult to get handles for leverage."[40] The stations had sought to lobby Congress against the free trade deal but overall it was seen as a good thing for the United States and that if it was to be enacted on a take-it-or-leave-it basis, and not subject to amendments, there was no way to hold up the deal on the broadcast issue itself.[41] Second, Arries felt that continuing the crusade was not cost effective, since the border stations were "not getting that much out of Canada" relative to the 1970's revenues and the legal and lobbying fees to wage the war.[42] In 1987, the stations in Buffalo, for example, had garnered only $6.4 million from Canadian advertising.[43] Coupled with this, Arries said, was that over the years the Canadian audience for the U.S. stations had been greatly reduced.[44] What had been a 42 percent penetration level had dropped to 30 percent, from sign-on to sign-off, with no American station having a share of the audience in Canada exceeding 15 percent.[45] Third, ownership of the stations pressing Canada had changed in recent years. They include the three network-affiliated stations in Buffalo, as well as the station in Bellingham. "The old gunfighters are not there," Arries commented.[46] Fourth, technology, to some degree, had passed, or bypassed, the border stations. Program reception in Canada no longer had to depend on the border stations' over-the-air signals, as Canada has developed sophisticated satellites, a massive cable system, a network to pick signals up in Detroit and Seattle and distribute them to the far north (CanCom), extensive use of VCRs, etc. Fifth, under these circumstances, the border stations were concerned over their ability to recapture the audience penetration they enjoyed in the 1970's, Arries said.[47]

In Canada during the summer of 1988, the government was weighing changes in its Broadcasting Act, including copyright protection for owners of U.S. programs whose shows are picked up by cable companies.[48] However, the broadcast provision of Bill C-58 was seen as essentially inviolable, according to Florian Sauvageau, cochairman of the Report of the Task Force on Broadcasting.[49]

SUMMARY

As depicted in the last four parts of this study, the U.S. border stations have mounted since 1976 a sustained, aggressive, and multifront campaign to pressure Canada to exempt broadcast advertising from Bill C-58, or, if that did not work, to force Canada to modify the bill. In a conservative estimate, the measure, through 1989 cost the border stations--principally the three in Buffalo and one in Washington--well in excess of $260 million in lost Canadian advertising.[50] The stations in the Buffalo market alone lost $75 to $100 million from 1976 to 1986.[51]

The economic motivation has fueled a variety of both negotiation maneuvers as well as retaliatory ones; the latter were invariably linked to the border stations seeking congressional or administration support to prevent Canada from getting something it wanted, unless relief on Bill C-58 was forthcoming. These tactics included the border stations' playing a major role in blocking, for more than four years, a tourist exemption for Canada, mirror legislation, unsuccessful efforts to curb importation of the sophisticated Canadian videotex system, Telidon, which had been tied to the proposed mirror legislation, and efforts to tie up the free trade talks.

Mirror legislation cost Canada some $5 million in lost American advertising revenue, but it is far short of the $20 million a year plus the border stations are losing. The border stations also proposed a number of what they viewed as compromises, for example, one was putting 20 percent of the Canadian revenue back into Canada as a television production fund. Nothing, however, budged Canada on Bill C-58. Canada has steadfastly viewed Bill C-58 as an internal matter, as having improved the viability of at least five Canadian television stations, and as part of the country's cultural policy.

With efforts to hold up the free trade pact ineffective, station ownership changed, and the Canadian audience decreased, due, in part, to advanced technology, with uncertain prospects of recapturing the audience in Canada that the border stations once enjoyed in the 1970's, combined with mounting legal and lobbying costs, the border stations in mid-1988 wound the war down.

NOTES

1. Alfred C. Cordon, border stations' counsel, letter to Leslie G. Arries, Jr., president of WIVB, Buffalo, July 28, 1980, p. 1.

2. Federal Register, vol. 45, no. 150, August 1, 1980, pp. S1173-74.

3. The same day as President Carter's memorandum, July 31, 1980, the Office of the U.S. Trade Representative announced its findings and Carter's

recommendation of mirror legislation (see Office of the U.S. Trade Representative press release, no. 328, July 31, 1980).

4.   Cordon, letter August 1, 1980, p. 1.   The State Department, which is represented on the Section 301 Committee, had been opposed to retaliation, the border stations understood.   Counsel reported that the State Department had then taken a decidedly negative view of the Section 301 complaint (see Bart Fisher, counsel's letter to border stations, May 4, 1979, p. 1).

5.   Allan R. O'Brien, border stations' counsel in Ottawa, Canada, letter, August 30, 1980, p. 1.

6.   Lawrence Martin, "U.S. Likely to Get a Mirror Law for TV-Ad Battle with Canada," Globe and Mail, July 31, 1980, p. 15.

7.   Wall Street Journal, "Retaliation Sought by Carter in Canada Border-TV Dispute," August 1, 1980, p. 4.   See also Canadian Press, "U.S. Retaliates against Canada in TV War," August 1, 1980.

8.   Cordon, letter to Robert Howard, president of Howard Publications, owners of WIVB, Buffalo, August 6, 1980.

9.   Congressional Record, message to Congress by President Carter, September 9, 1980, p. S12289.

10.   Bureau of National Affairs, "Taxation and Accounting," no. 178, September 11, 1980, p. 9.

11.   Jack Miller, "Broadcast war blasts Windsor station," Toronto Star, August 23, 1980, p. D-10.

12.   Ibid. See also Martin.

13.   Miller.

14.   Ibid.

15.   Bart Fisher, border stations' counsel, letter to Marcus Cohn, also counsel, January 9, 1981, p. 2.

16.   Ibid.

17.   Ibid.

18.   Responding to Carter's message, the first mirror bill (HR 8279) was sponsored by Representative John LaFalce, representative from the Buffalo area, on October 2, 1980.   Since it was introduced at the close of the 96th Congress, however, there was not time to consider it as the session ended.

19.   Congressional Record, message to Congress by President Reagan, February 2, 1982, p. S267.

20.   Conable's bill was cosponsored by representatives Jones, VanderJagt, Frenzel, Kemp, LaFalce, Nowak, and Swift.

21.   Danforth's bill was cosponsored by senators Moynihan, Bentsen, Wallop, Mitchell, Heinz, Symms, Cohen, Gorton and Jackson.

22.   Barber Conable, Congressional Record, introducing mirror legislation, December 14, 1981, p. E5821.

23.   Congressional Record, Reagan.

24.   Leslie G. Arries, Jr., in-person interview with author at WIVB, Buffalo, May 2, 1983.

25.   Nicholas P. Miller, counsel for the border stations, in a letter to Diana Lady Dougan, U.S. State Department, May 25, 1983.

26. William E. Brock, U.S. trade representative, in a letter to George Bush, president of U.S. Senate, August 3, 1983.   See also editorial in "Back at It," Broadcasting, August 29, 1983, p. 7.

27. "Bill Opposes Canada Law on TV Ads," Buffalo News, November 8, 1983, p. A-8.

28. Janet Graham, Canadian Department of External Affairs, general policy section; Silvia Gravel, Canadian Department of Communication, international relations section. In-person interviews by Barry Berlin in Ottawa, April 14 and 15, 1983.

29. "Washington Watch: Trade Bill," Broadcasting, November 5, 1984, p. 46. The bill is Section 245 of the Omnibus Trade and Tariff Act of 1984.

30. Leslie G. Arries, Jr., telephone interview with Barry Berlin, April 2, 1985.

31. In a report prepared for the Canadian Department of Communications, the tax advantage due to Bill C-58 was found to be $28 to $33 million in 1982. See Arthur Donner and Mel Kliman, "Television Advertising and the Income Tax Act: An Economic Analysis of Bill C-58," November 1983, p. 101. In 1984, researchers estimated that Bill C-58 increased net revenues of Canadian television stations and networks by $38.8 million. See Arthur W. Donner, "An Analysis of the Importance of U.S. TV Spillover, C-58 and Simulcasting Policies for the Revenues of Canadian TV Broadcasters," a study prepared for the Task Force on Broadcasting Policy, Minister of Supply Services, Ottawa, p. 460.

32. Gerald Lewis Caplan and Florian Sauvageau, cochairmen, Report of the Task Force on Broadcasting Policy, Minister of Supply Services, Ottawa, 1986, p. 461.

33. "Broadcasters Seek Resolution of Trade Dispute with Canada," Broadcasting, October 6, 1986, p. 60.

34. Jim Wright, Speaker of the U.S. House of Representatives, letter to Ambassador Clayton Yeutter, U.S. trade representative, August 7, 1987.

35. Senators Brock Adams, Alfonse D'Amato, John Heinz, William S. Cohen, Kent Conrad, Donald W. Riegle, Jr., Daniel J. Evans, and Quentin N. Burdick, letter to Clayton Yeutter, August 3, 1987.

36. Alfred C. Cordon letter to Thomas Howard of Howard Publications, owner of WIVB, Buffalo, January 7, 1988.

37. Arries, in-person interview with Barry Berlin, at the station, August 4, 1988.

38. There is some relief in the agreement, signed by President Reagan and Prime Minister Mulroney on January 2, 1988, for periodicals. Two measures would also help broadcasters in the United States, but not through tax relief. The first is a provision for copyright protection for owners of U.S. programs picked up for distribution by cable in Canada. The second is the reserved right of both countries to take retaliatory measures in response to actions affecting existing commercial rights. See The Canada-U.S. Free Trade Agreement, External Affairs, Ottawa, 1988, pp. 292-293.

39. Arries, 1988 interview.

40. Ibid.

41. Ibid.

42. Ibid.

43. Figures for 1987 provided by WIVB, Buffalo. Of the total, $500,000 was for WIVB (Channel 4); $650,000 for Channel 7; $1.3 million, for Channel 2; and $3.95 million for channels 29 and 49, two independent stations.

44. Arries, 1988 interview.

45. "Broadcasters Seek Resolution." Broadcasting.

46. Arries, 1988 interview.

47. Ibid.

48. Some new provisions went into effect January 1, 1990.

49. Florian Sauvageau, cochairman of the 1986 Report of the Task Force on Broadcasting Policy. In-person interview with Barry Berlin, in Quebec City, July 18, 1988.

50. The $240 million figure is derived from a loss of $20 million a year for twelve years, and is no doubt a low one because a scenario would want to take into account the growth in advertising revenue most years. In fact, a Canadian task force reported that in 1984, Bill C-58 increased net revenues of Canadian television stations and networks by $38.8 million. See Gerald Lewis Caplan and Florian Sauvageau, Report on the Task Force on Broadcasting Policy (Ottawa: Minister of Supply and Services Canada, 1986), p. 460. In addition, the amount of revenue lost through simultaneous substitution became substantial in the 1980's, and the border stations began to oppose it, as well as Bill C-58.

51. "Broadcasters Seek Resolution." Broadcasting.

Conclusions

The dispute has been waged by each side on two levels. The first is economic, with millions of dollars at stake. The second involves issues of culture and identity. Whereas border stations elevated the economic issue to one of free trade and free flow of information, Canada elevated the economic issue to one of cultural protectionism. In each case, the second rationale was largely only rhetoric that proved useful in the pursuit of the first objective.

The rationale for Canadian broadcast controls in general, and for the border dispute in particular, stems largely from Trojan horse concerns--the perception that the massive media spillover has caused a significant negative impact on Canadian culture and identity.

Analytical, impressionistic, and other critical perspectives generally find--and decry--homogenization and acculturation of Canadian culture by the U.S. media. A review of the empirical research, although relatively sparse, suggests to this writer limited effects--both negative and positive--in identity, tastes, values, attitudes, and beliefs.[1] The empirical studies do show significant support for cognitive effects, however.[2] Some critical scholars, it must be noted, disagree with a limited-effect scenario, contending that it is the cumulative effects that are negatively affecting the culture and the empirical studies do not measure long-term effect.[3]

Since empirical evidence that U.S. media penetration significantly affects Canadian culture in terms of attitudes, values, and beliefs, seems lacking, the media imperialism rationale for protectionist broadcasting measures is of suspect legitimacy, while a rationale of political rhetoric used to stir nationalistic feelings is strengthened.

Yet the central issue is whether Canadian public policies respecting commercial deletion and the tax legislation (Bill C-58) have been effective. Commercial deletion, which removed Canadian advertising from border stations' signals on a random basis but retained the programs, caused Canadian advertisers to fear they would not be getting the exposure they were paying for and to reduce their advertising expenditures. Commercial deletion acted primarily as a warning shot to the border stations on account of its brief duration. It put the stations on notice that Canada was very serious and was followed by Bill C-58.

Available data indicates that Bill C-58 certainly repatriated a sizeable portion of the $20 million that had been flowing south to the border stations. However, that was only part of the bill's stated objectives. The larger goal was ostensibly a cultural one: that the repatriated monies would develop Canada's culture and identity primarily through additional Canadian television programming, and the hiring of Canadian talent. The increased Canadian production failed to come to fruition. The repatriated revenue did help at least five Canadian television stations survive, but the bulk of the revenue remaining in Canada was used to purchase more U.S. programming.[4] Ironically, the problem of the extensive amount of American fare on Canadian television worsened thereby.

Measured in noneconomic terms, Canada may still be a long-term winner. Economic nationalism and cultural nationalism may have been strengthened by Canada's posturing. If so, then Canadian sovereignty has been strengthened. By the criterion of economic nationalism, Canada has gained control of its broadcast and cable systems through ownership and advertising; repatriation in the broadcasting field, compared to other industrial sectors, has been most effective. Advertising controls can be seen as a natural extension of the policy of "Canadaization" in general, and in broadcasting in particular. If, therefore, Bill C-58 has been beneficial to Canada, the benefit is in the ledger as an intangible, namely, integrity or sovereignty of the nation.

Canada, like a person, has a right to deal with its anxieties. But just as individuals need to consider how to deal with anxieties vis-a-vis others, so, too, does Canada. Commercial deletion, even as judged by Canadian commentators, was a crude, overly blunt, severe, and unfair way of adjudicating the problem. Although the Canadian supreme court ruled that commercial deletion authorization was within the power of the CRTC, the high court's attention focused primarily on whether the federal government or the provinces would control cable.

Bill C-58 was an improvement on commercial deletion, but it left inequities. For example, cable television systems in Canada reaped tremendous windfall profits by the uncompensated use of border stations' services.

The border stations were able to exercise influence on U.S. responses because they effectively used the options of persuasion open to them and spent more than $3 million in legal fees for litigation and lobbying.[5] They hired law firms in both Washington, D.C., and Ottawa, as well as a public relations firm in Washington. The border stations' counsel, the record shows, were industrious in pursuing the border stations' objectives and seemingly sought as many routes to their goals as seemed promising.

The border stations' retaliatory approach coincided with the political climate in Congress. Lobbying was effective partly because the special relationship between the two countries was changing, and the United States was embarking on a policy of retaliation that made linkage workable. Retaliation by Congress in the border dispute was not an isolated act, but part of an apparent policy change in the former special relationship. Retaliation was deployed in a number of instances of bilateral discord. The unfair trade practice finding is direct evidence of a change in the U.S.-Canada relationship. Previously no complaint under the trade measure had been acted on by a president. Despite commercial deletion and Bill C-58, the dispute would have died if Congress had not been receptive to the border stations' lobbying.

Canada has traditionally viewed communication and communication technology as political vehicles. The government elites and cultural nationalists often join forces on one side, while the private off-air broadcasters, cable companies, advertisers, and the Canadian mass audience, with its appetite for American fare, form the other side. In the United States, the issue was ultimately viewed as primarily a free trade and technical problem, and the broadcasters exerted political power because, as one border television station executive commented in an interview with this author, "We are not potato farmers. The politicians want our air time." In contrast, while litigation, lobbying, and especially linkage can be effective methods of redress, they can also further erode a relationship between two countries. The United States opted for retaliation in the border broadcast dispute in part because this method was being used politically with Canada in other areas of bilateral disagreements, from fishing rights to auto pacts. The problem with linkage is that it can, in the long run, cause more problems than it solves. Although the dispute appears to have been evidence of an emerging political approach between the two countries, both sides in this "war" may have lost more than either side gained.

Economic nationalism rationalized by Canada in the pursuit of cultural expression, unity, and identity, and manifested in protectionist practices, set off an international dispute, cost Canada more money than it gained, and, through the CRTC's authorization of Canadian cable companies to carry specific border station signals in the process of licensing the cable firms, resulted in proliferating the American cultural experience.[6]

In economic terms, the border stations, primarily the three network affiliates in Buffalo and a station in Bellingham, have lost more than $260 million over the last thirteen years and spent more than $3 million in legal fees to recover it. Canada, on the other hand, has regained much of that $260 million, but lost $400 million in tourist revenue over the four years that the border stations helped to block an exemption to Canada for conventions. Canada has most recently lost, through mirror legislation (the U.S. version of Canada's Bill C-58) $5 million a year in U.S. advertising revenue that had gone to two Canadian stations near Detroit. In any event, Canada may have gained sovereignty and integrity, for which no pricetag exists. Fears of a cultural invasion by American media sounded an alarm for the erosion of Canadian economic resources by U.S. border stations.

By the summer of 1988 the war had finally wound down; however, this case study suggests what may be a growing problem in addressing what rights a country has over broadcast signals crossing its border. The Canada-U.S. border war shows a need for a formal mechanism to adjudicate trans-border information flow problems. One possibility might be the creation of a U.S.-Canada telecommunication commission, which would provide a framework for establishing obligations on the part of stations on both sides of the border to respect the sovereignty and integrity of both countries.[7]

National borders alone cannot restrict information flow. Only a unified approach entered into by both countries can help prevent further battles from which neither side can retreat unharmed. Perhaps, such a mechanism may emerge ultimately as an offshoot in implementing the Free Trade Agreement.

NOTES

1. For empirical studies, see Vernon Sparkes, "TV Across the Canadian Border: Does It Matter?" Journal of Communication 27:4 (Autumn 1977); George A. Barnett and Thomas L. McPhail, "An Examination of the Relationship of United States Television and Identity," International Journal of Intercultural Relations, 4 (1980); David E. Payne and Andre H. Caron, "Anglo-Phone Canadian and American Mass Media: Uses and Effects on Quebec Adults," Communication Research 9, no. 1 (January 1982); Earl Beattie, "In Canada's Centennial Year, United States Mass Media Probed," Journalism Quarterly 44 (1967); J. K. Skipper, "Musical Manifestation and American Theses," Canadian Journal of Sociology 1 (1975); C. Crawford and J. Curtis, "English Canadian-American Differences in Value Orientation: Survey Comparisons Bearing on Lipset's Thesis," Studies in Comparative International Development 304:23-44 (1979); Eugene Tate and Stuart H. Surlin, "Agreement with Opinionated TV Characters Across Cultures," Journalism Quarterly 53 (1976); David E. Payne and Andre H. Caron, "Mass Media

Interpersonal and Social Background Influences in Two Canadian and American Settings," Canadian Journal of Communication 9:4 (1983); Stephen J. Arnold and Douglas J. Tigert, "Canadians and Americans: A Comparative Analysis," International Journal of Comparative Sociology 15 (1974); Douglas Baer and James Winter, "American Media and Attitudes Regarding Government in a Canadian Border Community," Canadian Journal of Communication 10:1 (1983); Paul M. Sniderman, Joseph F. Fletcher, Peter H. Russell, Phillip E. Tetlock, "Liberty, Authority and Community: Civil Liberties and the Canadian Political Culture," paper presented at the annual meetings of the Canadian Political Science Association and the Canadian Law and Society Association, University of Windsor, June 9, 1988; Eugene D. Tate and Larry F. Trach, "The Effects of United States Television Programs upon Canadian Beliefs about Legal Procedure, Canadian Journal of Communication 6:4 (1980); James Curtis and Ronald D. Lambert, "Culture and Social Organization," in Sociology, edited by Robert Hagedorn (Toronto: Holt, Rinehart & Winston, 1980); Stuart H. Surlin and Barry Berlin, "Canadian and U.S. Perceptions of TV Values: Cultural Freedom or Domination?" Paper presented at the Association for Education in Journalism and Mass Communication conference, August 1989, in Washington, D.C.

2. Ibid.

3. Cess J. Hamelink, Cultural Autonomy in Global Communications (New York: Longman, 1983), for example, asserts that countries need relative cultural autonomy to avoid what he terms "cultural synchronization." See Seymour Martin Lipset, "Canada and the United States: The Cultural Dimension," in Charles F. Doran and John H. Sigler, eds., Canada and the United States (Englewood Cliffs, N.J.: Prentice Hall, 1985).

4. Arthur Donner and Fred Lazar, The Impact of the 1976 Income Tax Amendment on United States and Canadian TV Broadcasters, January 1979, pp. 111-19. See also Arthur Donner and Mel Kliman, "The Effect of Section 19.1 of the Income Tax Act on Television Advertising," The Canadian Journal 32, no. 6 (November-December 1984).

5. Leslie G. Arries, Jr., president of WIVB, Buffalo. Legal fee estimate made during in-person interview with author, May 2, 1983.

6. By early 1982, cable was reaching 58.9 percent of Canadian homes. See CBC Annual Report, 1982-82, Ottawa, p. 49.

7. See Theodore Hagelin and Hudson Janisch, "The Border Broadcasting Dispute in Context,"   paper submitted for a conference on Canada-U.S. telecommunications issues at the Center for Inter-American Relations in New York City, April 15, 1983.

Selected Bibliography

Applebaum, Louis, and Herbert, Jacques. <u>Report of the Federal
    Cultural Policy Review Committee</u>. Ottawa: Canadian
    Government Publishing Center, 1982.
Audley, Paul. <u>Canada's Cultural Industries: Broadcasting, Publishing,
    Records and Film</u>. Toronto: James Lorimer & Co., 1983.
Barnett, George A., and McPhail, Thomas L. "An Examination of the
    Relationship of United States Television and Canadian
    Identity." <u>International Journal of Intercultural Relations</u>.
    Vol. 4, 1980.
Beattie, Earl. "In Canada's Centennial Year, United States Mass
    Media Influence Probed." <u>Journalism Quarterly</u>. Vol. 44,
    1967.
"Bill Opposes Canada Law on TV Ads." <u>Buffalo News</u>, November 8,
    1983.
"Broadcasters Seek Resolution of Trade Dispute with Canada."
    <u>Broadcasting</u>, October 16, 1986.
Broadcasting Act of 1968, Sect. 1, Subsection 2(g) Ottawa: Queen's
    Printer.
Brown, Les. "Buffalo TV Plans A 'Jam' to Canada." <u>New York
    Times</u>, (November 18, 1975):67.
<u>Capital Cities Communications, Inc., et al.</u> v. <u>Canadian Radio-
    Television Commission et al</u>. (1974) 52 D.L.R. 3d 415.
    _____. 8 D.L.R. 3d 69-09, November 30, 1977.
Caplan, Gerald Lewis, and Sauvageau, Florian. <u>Report of the Task
    Force on Broadcasting Policy</u>. Ottawa: Minister of Supply
    Services, 1986.

Clarkson, Stephen. <u>Canada and the Reagan Challenge: Crisis in Canadian-American Relationship</u>. Toronto: James Lorimer & Co., 1982.

"A Confrontation with Canada over TV Ads." <u>Business Week</u>. (November 6, 1978):142.

Complaint filed pursuant to Section 301 of the Trade Act of 1974. The Section 301 Committee of the Office of the Special Representative for Trade Negotiations, Washington, D.C., August 29, 1978.

"Coping with Canada." <u>Broadcasting</u> (September 4, 1978):66.

Crean, S. M. <u>Who's Afraid of Canadian Culture?</u> Don Mills, Ontario: General Publishing Company, 1976.

CRTC. <u>Annual Report</u> (1981-82). Minister of supply and services Canada, Ottawa.

_____. (1972). Decisions 74-100; 74-101; 74-102.

_____. (1977). "Public Announcement: Commercial Cultures Delegation," Guy Lafebvre, secretary general, January 21.

_____. (1978). <u>Special Report on Broadcasting in Canada, 1968-1978: Main Points</u>. March 12.

_____. (1983). Policy statement on Canadian content in television. Notice 83-18, January 31.

<u>Cultures in Collision: The Interaction of Canadian and U.S. Television Broadcast Policies</u>. New York: Praeger, 1984.

Curtis, John M., and Moroz, Andrew R. "Introduction: A New Relationship," <u>Canadian Public Policy</u>, special supplement on Canadian-U.S. trade and policy issues. October, 1982.

Davey, Keith, "Freedom, Responsibility, Prospects for the Future," an address at an Association for Education in Journalism convention, August 18, 1975. Speech published in proceedings of that convention: <u>Border Impact: The Mass Media and Canadian Identity</u>. Brookings, S.D.: Department of Journalism and Mass Communication, South Dakota State University, March, 1976.

Debates of the [Canadian] Senate (1976), 1st session, 30th Parliament, vol. 123, no. 179, April 6.

_____. (1976), 1st session, 30th Parliament, vol. 123, no. 165, March 10.

_____. (1976), 1st session, 30th Parliament, vol. 123, no. 162, March 3.

_____. (1976), 1st session, 30th Parliament, vol. 123, no. 207, June 29.

Department of Communication, Canada. <u>Vital Links: Canadian Cultural Industries</u>. Ottawa: Ministry of Supply Services, 1987.

Dickey, John Sloane. <u>Canada and the American Presence</u>. New York: New York University Press, 1975.

Donner, Arthur and Lazar, Fred. The Impact of the 1976 Income Tax Amendment on United States and Canadian TV Broadcasters (January, 1979):1-30.

Eaman, Ross A. The Media Society: Basic Issues and Controversies.
    Toronto: Butterworths, 1987.
Elkin, Frederick. "Communications Media and Identity Formation in
    Canada," in Communications in Canadian Society, ed.
    Benjamin D. Singer. Toronto: Copp Clark, 1975.
Fayerweather, John. The Mercantile Bank Affair. New York: New
    York University Press, 1974.
Fox, Francis. Minister of Communications, Towards a New National
    Broadcast Policy. Ottawa: Minister of Supply Services,
    Canada. Document undated but made public in March, 1983.
Frey, Frederick W. "Communication and Development," in
    Handbook of Communication, ed. Ithiel de Sola Pool.
    Chicago: Rand McNally, 1973.
Ganley, O. H. "Political Aspects of Communications and
    Information," in The Information Society, 1981.
Gerbner, George. Mass Media Policies in Changing Cultures. New
    York: John Wiley and Sons, 1977.
_____. "Comparative Cultural Indicators," in Mass Media Policies
    in Changing Cultures, ed. George Gerbner, New York: John
    Wiley and Sons, 1988.
Gray, John. "Broadcasting Policy Forgets Cultural Concerns." Globe
    and Mail, March 5, 1983.
Hagelin, Theodore and Janisch, Hudson. The Border Broadcasting
    Dispute in Context. A paper submitted for the conference on
    Canada-United States Telecommunications Issues at the
    Center for Inter-American Relations. March 11, 1983.
Howell, W. J., Jr. World Broadcasting in the Age of the Satellite.
    Norwood, N.J.: Ablex Publishing, 1986.
Johnson, A. W. President of the Canadian Broadcast Corp. (CBC), in
    statement entitled "Touchstone for the CBC," June, 1977.
Kent, Tom L. The Royal Commission on Newspapers. Hull, Quebec:
    Minister of Supply Services, Canada, 1981.
King, John. "Restrictions on Foreign Conventions Eased, U.S. Move
    Worth Millions to Canada," Globe and Mail (January 28,
    1978):12.
Lee, Chin-Chuan. Media Imperialism Reconsidered: The
    Homogenizing of Television Culture. Beverly Hills, Calif.:
    Sage Publications, 1979.
Lipset, Seymour Martin. North American Cultures: Values and
    Institutions in Canada and the United States. Orono, Me.:
    Borderlands Monograph Series, University of Maine, 1990.
Lorimer, Rowland M. and McNulty, Jean. Mass Communication in
    Canada. Toronto: McClelland and Stewart, 1987.
_____. and Wilson, Donald C. Communication Canada: Issues in
    Broadcasting and New Technologies. Toronto: Kagan and
    Woo, 1988.
Lu Duc, Don R. "Cable TV Control in Canada: A Comparative
    Study," Journal of Broadcasting 20:4 (Fall, 1976).

Madden, John C. Videotex in Canada. Hull, Quebec: Minister of
        Supply Services Canada, 1979.
Martin, Lawrence. "Block Canadian Shows, U.S. Urged," Globe and
        Mail (November 30, 1978):10.
_____ "U.S. Likely to Get a Mirror Law for TV-Ad Battle with
        Canada," Globe and Mail (July 31, 1980).
Miller, Jack. "Buffalo-TV Stations Threatened to Black Out Canada,"
        Toronto Star (February 6, 1975):1.
_____ "Border War Cools: End Hinted to United States Ad Cuts
        from Cable TV." Toronto Star (October 7, 1976):A7.
_____ "Supreme Court Tries to Settle TV Border War," Toronto
        Star (January 26, 1977).
_____ "Broadcast War Blasts Windsor Station," Toronto Star
        (August 23, 1980).
_____ "Pay-TV Freebies Forbidden," The Saturday (Toronto) Star
        (January 15, 1983).
Miller, Robert E. "The CRTC: Guardian of the Canadian Identity,"
        Journal of Broadcasting 172 (Spring 1973):194.
Morton, William L. The Canadian Identity. Madison, Wis.: The
        University of Wisconsin Press, 1965.
Nielsen, Richard P. and Nielsen, Angela, B. "Canadian TV Content
        Regulation and U.S. Cultural 'Overflow'," Journal of
        Broadcasting 20:4 (Fall 1976).
O'Toole, Lawrence. "Rogers Cable Claims No Danger in Buffalo
        Plan to Cut Off Signals," Toronto Star (February 7, 1975):35.
Payne, David E. and Caron, Andre H. "Anglo-Phone Canadian and
        American Mass Media: Uses and Effects on Quebec Adults."
        Communication Research 9, no. 1, January 1982.
Peers, Frank W. The Politics of Canadian Broadcasting 1920-1951.
        Toronto: University of Toronto Press, 1969.
_____ The Public Eye: Television and the Politics of Canadian
        Broadcasting, 1952-1968. Toronto: University of Toronto
        Press, 1979.
_____ "Canada and the United States: Comparative Origins and
        Approaches to Broadcast Policy." A paper prepared for
        delivery at a conference, "Canada-United States: The
        Telecommunication Issue," in New York City, March 11, 1983.
Pool, I. de Sola. "Direct Broadcasting Satellites and the Integrity of
        National Culture," in Control of the Direct Broadcast Satellite:
        Values in Conflict. Palo Alto, Calif.: Aspen Institute Program
        on Communication and Society, 1974.
Powell, Roland. "United States Optimistic in Canadian Talks on
        Deletion of TV Commercials," Buffalo Evening News
        (November 24, 1976):55.
_____ "Canada Bars Talks on Tax Deduction for U.S. TV Ads,"
        Buffalo Evening News (March, 14, 1979):40.
_____ "Retaliation Sought by Carter in Canada Border-TV
        Dispute," Wall Street Journal, August 1980.

Rotstein, Abraham. "Canada: The New Nationalism." Foreign
    Affairs 55 (October, 1976):11.
Saywell, John. Canada Past and Present. Toronto: Clark, Irwin &
    Co., 1975.
Section 301 (2) of the Trade Act of 1974 (1974), 19 USC 2411.
Siegel, Arthur. Politics and the Media in Canada. Toronto:
    McGraw-Hill Ryerson, 1983.
Skipper, J. K., Jr. "Musical Tastes of Canadian and American College
    Students: An Examination of the Manifestation and American
    Theses." Canadian Journal of Sociology, 1975.
Sparkes, Vernon. "Community Cablecasting in the U.S. and Canada:
    Different Approaches to a Common Objective." Journal of
    Broadcasting, 20:4 (1976).
_____. "TV across the Canadian Border: Does It Matter?" Journal
    of Broadcasting 27:4 (Autumn 1977).
Surlin, Stuart H. and Berlin, Barry. "Canadian and U.S. Perceptions
    of TV Values: Cultural Freedom or Domination?" Paper
    presented at the Association for Education in Journalism and
    Mass Communication, Washington, D.C., August 1989.
Swinton, Katherine. Advertising and Canadian Cable Television: A
    Problem in International Communications Law, 15 Osgoode
    Hall Law Journal, December, 1977.
"Thieving," an editorial Globe and Mail (September 26, 1975):15.
Gray, John. "Broadcasting Policy Forgets Cultural Concerns." Globe
    and Mail, Toronto, March 5, 1983.
Toffler, Alvin. "Mass Media: A Force in Identity Change," in
    Communications in Canadian Society, ed. Benjamin D. Singer.
    Toronto: Copp Clark, 1977.
Togood, Alex. "The Canadian Broadcasting System: Search for a
    Definition," Journalism Quarterly 48, Summer 1971.
"Washington Watch: Trade Bill," Broadcasting, November 5, 1984.
Weiss, Elaine F. "Tearing the Fabric of Canada: The Broadcast
    Media and Canadian Identity," paper presented at the annual
    meeting of the Association for Education in Journalism, San
    Diego, August 18-21, 1974.
Znaimer, Moses. President, CITY-TV, Toronto. "The Border Battle
    Intensifies Despite Bill C-58," Globe and Mail (November 5,
    1975):6.

Index

About the Author

BARRY BERLIN is an Associate Professor in the Communication Department at Canisius College, Buffalo, New York. A former print journalist, Dr. Berlin teaches a course on Canadian media and culture and his research interests have focused on the media in both the United States and Canada.